WHN

When New York City Went Country

Also by the author

Pittsburgh's Golden Age of Radio

WHN

When New York City Went Country

TO MIKE,
THANKS FOR ALL YOUR HELP
WITH THE WHN REUNION
ON WFDU

ED SALAMON

Archer Books
Los Angeles

Published in 2013 in the United States by
Archer Books
P. O. Box 1254
Santa Maria, CA 93456
www.archer-books.com — jtcimag@archer-books.com

First Edition

Printed in the United States

Cover design: JTC Imagineering

ISBN 978-1-931122-26-9

Library of Congress Cataloging-in-Publication Data

TK

Dedicated to the millions of radio listeners who tuned in to WHN for country music and made this story possible.

TABLE OF CONTENTS

INTRODUCTION

"None of the success would have happened without the best and brightest broadcast professionals who had a passion for the greatest station they could produce, the second biggest radio station in all the world . . . WHN"
—Neil Rockoff, WHN General Manager (1975-1977)

Visitors from Nashville were often surprised when they got into a taxi at a New York airport in the 1970s and 80s and found that the cab driver may have been wearing a turban, but was listening to a country music radio station. WHN's audience didn't fit the country stereotype; it mirrored the diverse population of New York City.

WHN's programming was "crowd sourced"; the listeners determined which songs were played and how often through systems of call-out research and requests. Therefore, the station's playlist was often at odds with the music that was being promoted to country music radio by Nashville based labels, even though those same labels did benefit when WHN sold enough country records to interest Top 40 stations in adding them. Likewise, WHN embraced a wide variety of records with the country sound and opened the doors to country radio to a lot of artists who, without a Nashville base, would not otherwise have been heard on the format. WHN's broader definition of country music prevailed.

For example, though most country stations initially shunned the Eagles, they were a core WHN artist and their sound became pervasive in country music of the 80s and 90s.

Thanks to all of those who encouraged me to memorialize the story of the most listened to country music radio station of all time. I especially appreciate those who have contributed through interviews and correspondence, including Dan Abernathy, Duane Allen, Lee Arnold, Alan Colmes, Charlie Cook, Jeff Cook, Charlie Daniels, Del De Montreux, Jim Duncan, Frank D'Elia, Paul Evans, Mike Fitzgerald, Larry Gatlin, Robert Gordon, Douglas E. Hall, Peter Kanze, Ian Karr, Larry Kenney, Barry Kluger, Gene Ladd, Dale Pon, J. J. Ramey, Neil Rockoff, Howie Rose, Jessie Scott, Joe Stampley, Susan Storms, Dan Taylor, Bernie Wagenblast, Steve Warren, Sheila York and Ellen Zucker.

Special thanks to WHN's other program directors: Joel Raab, Moon Mullins and Gary Havens, and music director Pam Green.

Thanks to Katy Salamon for her editing and John Taylor-Convery at Archer Books, without whom this book would not have been possible.

This book contains the best of my recollection and the recollections of those who contributed. I realize that those involved may recall differently, as even some of those interviewed have conflicting memories. I sorted those out as best I could. Likewise, I'm sure there are items that some feel are meaningful that I have left out. I apologize in advance.

Ratings and chart information are from secondary sources such as memos, ads and press reports. We have intentionally avoided publishing specific ratings or record chart data, which may fall under copyright.

All photos are from the author's collection, unless otherwise credited.

PROLOGUE

WHN (currently WEPN) is arguably the oldest radio station consistently licensed to New York City. Of the two other contenders, WABC (formerly WJZ), was licensed to Bound Brook, New Jersey in the 1920s; WNBC (formerly WEAF), the first radio station in Manhattan, signed on the following month.

WHN first signed on in February 1922 at 360 meters on the AM dial at the power of 15 watts with a program of piano rolls, records and live piano music by Joseph Stroehlein, a music store proprietor who served as the station's first announcer and program director. WHN was licensed to George Schubel, founder and publisher of the *Ridgewood Times* in Queens, New York. WHN shared operating time with station WJZ, which was owned by Westinghouse Electric and Manufacturing Company. At the time, WHN was one of only 30 commercially licensed broadcast stations in the United States and the only one in Queens County. The original studio was in the Ridgewood Chamber Of Commerce meeting room. Like all stations at the time, it operated commercial free and at variable hours.

Schubel believed that if soliciting advertising was permitted, and if there were a sufficient number of people with radios, it would be possible for a radio station to sell advertising the same as a newspaper in order to make it a business. In August 1922, the U.S. Department of Commerce changed its regulation and permitted radio stations to broadcast commercials. With WHN now permitted to solicit advertising, George Schubel invested in a more powerful transmitter of 50 watts.

On July 28, 1923, Schubel entered into an agreement with Loew's Theaters to provide WHN's programming. Loew's relocated the station's offices to 1540 Broadway. Nils Thor Granlund, publicist for Loew's, became WHN's chief announcer, under the air name NTG. On August 9th, the station celebrated its new management with a gala broadcast featuring Irving Berlin, Eddie Cantor and George M. Cohan. Shortly after WHN's move to Manhattan, WJZ moved there from Newark, New Jersey, and the U.S. Department of Commerce assigned them a new wavelength of 455 (equivalent to a frequency of 660), replacing their use of the 360-meter wavelength. WHN's power was increased to 500 watts. It would be doubled to 1,000 watts one year later. As part of the deal, Schubel accepted a 10-year contract to join the Loew's Organization as general manager of stations WHN and WPSP in Palisades Park, New Jersey, which Loew's had acquired.

In 1924, AT&T (the American Telephone & Telegraph Company), which owned New York station WEAF, filed suit against WHN. AT&T contended that WHN had no right to sell commercial time, since it had never been granted a license to operate commercially from AT&T for what it termed "toll broadcasting." This was based on the fact that AT&T's patents covered some circuitry found in nearly all radio equipment. The case was later settled out of court. AT&T would receive a license fee of $1500 from WHN.

In 1927, WHN changed frequency to 760 AM. In October 1928, WHN was sold to Loew's. The licensee became the Marcus Loew Booking Agency. Loew's changed the dial position to 1010 and was able to increase power to 5,000 watts. Loew's Theater owner, Marcus Loew, had also purchased Metro Pictures Corporation, Goldwyn Pictures and Louis B.

Mayer Pictures to assure a steady supply of films for his theaters, eventually combining them into Metro-Goldwyn-Mayer, or MGM. WHN's slogan was "The Voice of the Great White Way." Many performers would spontaneously drop in on programs when they were in the area.

In August of 1933, George Schubel's contract with the Loew's Organization expired. It apparently was not renewed.

On January 9, 1934, WHN absorbed its share-time radio partners and broadcast full-time on 1010 AM.

These were the days before format radio, and it was customary for stations to carry a variety of talk and music programming. In the 1930s WHN's programming included the *WHN Barn Dance,* which was said to have rivaled the *Grand Ole Opry.* Tex Ritter was the host and featured singer before becoming a motion picture star. Other performers included Gene Autry, The Phelps Brothers and Ray Whitley.

WHN was an affiliate of the Mutual Broadcasting System and carried network programming which was not carried by Mutual's flagship station, WOR. The most notable were *Top of the News,* featuring newspaper columnist Fulton Lewis, Jr., which was so successful it was taken by WOR after six months.

WHN was managed for Lowe's by Edward "Major" Bowes. *Major Bowes' Original Amateur Hour*, which began at the Capitol Theater that Bowes also managed, started airing on WHN in 1934. The following year it was broadcast on network radio as part of NBC's *Chase and Sanborn Hour.* On September 17, 1936, the show moved to the CBS Radio Network, where it stayed for the remainder of its run on radio in 1952. It was hosted by Ted Mack after Bowes death.

In an early example of cross promotion, a WHN microphone appeared in the 1935 Marx Brothers' film, *A Night at the Opera.* It was the first movie the comedians made for MGM, subsequent to their departure from Paramount.

Country singer Red River Dave McEnery began performing

on NYC's WHN radio in 1938. He was best known for his story songs about news events, such as his 1941 recording, "Amelia Earhart's Last Flight."

On December 1, 1941, WHN's dial position was again changed, this time to 1050, and the power increased to 50,000 watts with a directional signal.

Brooklyn Dodgers baseball moved to WHN from WOR in 1942, with Red Barber at Ebbets Field. Giants football and Rangers hockey were also heard, and Marty Glickman perfected the art of describing a basketball game with the New York Knicks on WHN.

Sister station WHN-FM went on the air on Monday, June 1, 1943. Originally broadcasting at 46.3 megacycles, with programming consisting mostly of transcribed classical and semi classical music. In 1946, the frequency was relocated to 100.3 when the FM dial was moved to 88.1-105.9. It was an often told story at WHN that, during the rise of FM in the 1970s, Lowe's, not seeing any future for FM broadcasting, turned the license back in to the federal government. That 100.3 frequency would most famously be home to Z-100.

Elsewhere on the New York dial, country performers Shorty and Smokey Warren moved their show to Newark's WAAT from Phoenix, Arizona about 1941. After World War II, Dave Miller was playing country records on WAAT, as was Don Larkin. In the late 50s, Don's *Hometown Frolics* show moved to WNTA, also in Newark. In a 1956 poll by *Country & Western Jamboree* magazine, Larkin finished No. 2 as the "Favorite Local Radio Disc Jockey" behind WSM Nashville's T. Tommy (Cutrer).

In 1946, *Billboard* magazine reported that Davy Denny, a new cowboy singing star, was heard on WHN.

WHN pioneered sports talk radio when Marty Glickman first took questions on air. Glickman relayed the callers' comments to his audience since the technology didn't yet exist to broadcast phone calls.

WHN: When New York City Went Country

On September 15, 1948, WHN changed call letters to WMGM. The call letter change was to promote the station's relationship with the co-owned MGM studio and to prepare for Metro-Golden-Mayer's entry into radio syndication the following year. WHN moved from Loew's State Theatre to "new million-dollar studios" at 711 5th Ave., the old NBC location. As an MGM affiliate, WHN carried MGM radio dramas and comedies featuring MGM stars and produced programs transcribed to discs in their Hollywood studio for airplay on local radio affiliates. Shows including *Dr. Kildare, Crime Does Not Pay, Adventures of Masie featuring Ann Southern* and *MGM Theater of the Air* utilized material already recorded by MGM. New programming included *Hollywood, USA*, a celebrity interview series with Paula Stone. This arrangement lasted until the early 50s.

WHN local programming included *Newsreel Theatre,* an all news show for an hour from 6:00 to 7:00 am, followed by Robert Q. Lewis with his record show till 9:00 am. In 1950, Robert Q. Lewis left for CBS and he was succeeded in the morning slot by Ted Brown and the Redhead (his real-life wife, Rhoda Brown). Actress Sylvia Miles later played the Redhead.

In the spring of 1957, Jerry Marshall departed WNEW's *Make Believe Ballroom* to join the station. WHN began to rely more on local programming with the addition of personalities including Dick DeFreitas, Norm Tulin (aka Norm Stevens), Bill Silbert, Ed Stokes and Phil Goulding (brother of Ray Goulding of the Bob and Ray comedy team). Vaudevillians Blossom Seeley and Benny Fields had their own show and Harold Peary, the actor who created, and later abandoned, "The Great Gildersleeve" also become a WMGM deejay.

Meanwhile, further up the dial, RCA singing star Rosalie Allen hosted a country music show, *Prairie Stars* on New York station WOV in the late 40s and early 50s.

In 1957, WMGM moved to 400 Park Avenue, the location from which it would later begin its country programming. The station adopted a Top 40 format to compete with WINS. The air staff included Ted Brown and the Redhead, Jerry Marshall, Peter Tripp, Norm Stevens, Dick Shephard, Bob Lewis, Ed Stokes and Bob Callen.

Tripp was named in the payola scandal. In May of 1960, he was charged, along with several other New York disc jockeys, with playing particular records in return for gifts from record companies. Despite his claim that he "never took a dime from anyone," he was found guilty on commercial bribery, receiving a $500 fine and a six-month suspended sentence. In the wake of the payola scandals, Mike Lawrence took over Tripp's programs and WHN music director Joe Saccone was replaced by WINS music director Rick Sklar.

In 1960, WMGM began broadcasting 24 hours a day. One of the city's first female deejays, Bea Kalmus, and Bill Edmonds moved into the 2:30-5:00 am time slot, carrying over the contemporary daytime sound.

Crowell-Collier publishing company announced it would buy WMGM for $11 million, but the FCC denied the application, citing Crowell-Collier's mismanagement of its Los Angeles station, KFWB.

In 1962, WMGM was sold to George B. Storer for $10,950,000. Despite the fact that Storer owned Top 40 stations WIBG in Philadelphia and WJBK in Detroit, the company changed WMGM's format to "Sound of Music, Total Information, News" and its call letters back to WHN on February 28, 1962. Deejay Bob Callan played the last rock record, "Peppermint Twist" by Joey Dee. John C. Moeler of WIBG was brought in as general manager.

The format switch occurred during a party in the Grand Ballroom of the Waldorf Astoria Hotel with music provided by Hugo Winterhalter, The Ray Charles Singers and the Kirby Stone Four. In the following years, WHN programmed album tracks and avoided pop hits completely. The radio comedy team of Bob (Elliott) and Ray (Goulding) was hired to do an afternoon show.

By 1965, WHN had an eleven man news department under Mike Prelee, who came from WJW in Cleveland when WHN was WMGM. At that point, their program director was Ted Schneider and music director Graham Slater.

On September 15, 1965, WJRZ radio (formerly WAAT), which covered the New York metropolitan area from Newark, New Jersey, became the first area station to switch to an all-country format. That format lasted on that station until May 17, 1971.

In May 1966, WHN switched to an easy listening format under program director Graham Slater. WHN now played hit singles that weren't rock n' roll, by artists including Eddy Arnold, Herb Alpert and the Tijuana Brass, Jack Jones, Jerry Vale, Lanie Kazan and Bobby Darin. Slater was quoted as saying that a month earlier he would have never considered those artists. There had been rumors that the station would change format to country music instead.

By 1968 Marv Albert was a WHN sportscaster.

By the early 1970s, under program director Alan Hotlen, WHN had added some soft rock selections and a midday talk and music show, *Feminine Forum*. WHN was the flagship station of the Mets, Nets and Islanders. In 1970, WHN brought in another established wake-up man, Herb Oscar Anderson. Alan Kalter, later to be the announcer on *The Late Show with David Letterman*, was WHN's production director. Engineer Frank D'Elia recalls that when he started at WHN in 1972, it was the flagship station of Nets basketball, Islanders hockey and Mets baseball, and the WHN sports director was Bill Mazur.

CHAPTER ONE
1973

"Country Sunshine" – Dottie West (1973)

In 1973, conventional industry wisdom was that a country radio station could not be successful in the New York market.

In early January, WHN president John Sullivan, Storer national program director Chuck Renwick and WHN program director Alan Hotlen made a stealth trip to Nashville to consult with the Country Music Association about a format change to country. Hotlen remembers checking into the Holiday Inn Vanderbilt and hearing Eddy Arnold's unmistakable voice saying, "Alan, what are YOU doing here?" Arnold had met Hotlen during the time when his songs were crossing over to pop radio and never forgot him. Renwick and Hotlen soon realized that their cover was blown, and the industry rumor mill began to buzz.

Later that month, when WHN announced that the station was changing its format to country, it was important enough that it was front page news in *Billboard* magazine. In sharp contrast to the rural images of country music portrayed on the recent CBS-TV series *Hee Haw,* the station made the announcement to its advertisers at The Sign Of The Dove, a lavish restaurant on the northwest corner of Third Avenue and 65th Street. WHN general manager John Sullivan, as always impeccably attired in a blazer from Sulka, an exclusive men's haberdashery, made the announcement. Hotlen recalls the response as being "a round of indifference."

Storer national program director Chuck Renwick took an extended leave from his position as general manager of Storer's WJW, Cleveland, and was brought in to oversee the format transition. Sullivan was quoted saying that as many of the air staff as possible would be retained and that their midday, two-way talk program, *Feminine Forum*, would remain and incorporate country music. *Feminine Forum* had started as a two-way talk show hosted by Bill Ballance on Storer's KGBS, Los Angeles. Aimed at "housewives," its sexual topics aroused controversy well before any of radio's shock jocks. Nevertheless, the concept was so successful that Storer replicated it with local hosts in other markets.

Hotlen recalls that Bob Fitzsimmons was slated to be the morning personality on the country format, but he could not come to terms with Sullivan on a deal, so Fitzsimmons resigned shortly before the format change. Since Fitzsimmons and Hotlen had both worked together at WPEN, Hotlen was dispatched to Fitzsimmons' home to try to save the deal to no avail. Hotlen remembers Fitzsimmons saying that "there is nothing like two Irishmen at loggerheads," referring to his conversation with Sullivan. Hotlen then asked Jack Spector to step in at the last moment and Spector graciously agreed to host WHN's morning show, knowing he was not the station's first choice. Music director Corrine Baldassano left to become music director at WPLJ and was replaced by assistant music director Bob Russo.

The switch to country came at 5:45 am on February 26th, with Les Davis ending WHN's middle of the road format and Jack Spector, calling himself "The Kosher Cowboy From Coney Island," introducing the George Jones classic "The Race Is On." The station billed itself as "Easy Lovin' Country" and used a butterfly in its subway and newspaper advertising.

In a *New York Times* article that day, "WHN Joins Camp of

Country Music," Hotlen was quoted. "There is a back-to-the-soil feeling among urbanites now-a-days. People are ecology conscious. They long for simple days when music reflected love and loneliness and death and going to jail, the stuff country music is about."

The initial lineup for country WHN was Jack Spector (mornings), Bruce Bradley (middays), Bob Jones (early afternoon), Lee Arnold (afternoon drive), Del De Montreux (evenings), Stan Martin (overnight) and Les Davis (weekends). Lee Arnold was the only talent with significant country radio experience. He had been music director of WJRZ, a fulltime country station from Hackensack, New Jersey, which covered the New York market. Lee had already been working overnights at WHN. Jack Spector, best known as one of the WMCA Good Guys, had joined the station the previous year. Bruce Bradley, a 60s staple on WBZ, Boston, remained in middays. Bob Jones, like Bruce, had hosted the *Feminine Form* show. De Montreux had been on the air weekends at WHN. Stan Martin had been at WPIX-FM. When the air shifts were set, *Feminine Forum* had disappeared from the schedule.

Del De Montreux had been hired by WHN as an intern the previous year after leaving the Army. He was originally put in charge of booking guests for Bill Mazur's *Sports Roundtable* from the Oak Room of the Plaza Hotel. When WHN's then afternoon air personality, Bob Fitzsimmons, discovered that Del was Del Curtis, who had worked in radio in the Youngstown area at the same time as he did, he told the program director that he should be on the air. Del had worked on the air at WEIR in Steubenville, Ohio and at KDKA in Pittsburgh as Del Curtis while attending the College of St. Steubenville. In Youngstown, De Montreux also hosted WSTV-TV's *Channel 9 Teen Time* dance show. In 1968, he joined the Army, where he worked in radio and television on the Southern Command Network in Panama. Del recalls that he was fired by Alan Hotlen who didn't feel he could make the switch to country, but was rehired by new program director Ruth Meyer one week later. Meyer, who had been on site acting as a consultant during the format change, replaced Hotlen in March. Hotlen returned to his hometown of Philadelphia as director of news and programming at WCAU-AM.

Ruth Meyer had worked at WHB with Top 40 radio pioneer Todd Storz before achieving success as program director of New York Top 40 station WMCA. Ruth hired some of her WMCA Good Guys to become country radio personalities; Dan Daniel replaced Bob Jones and Joe O'Brien replaced Les Davis for weekends. Fellow Good Guys Joe O'Brien, Ed Baer and Dean Anthony were later added to the schedule for part time and fill in. Former WMCA newsman Steve Powers also joined WHN. Engineer Frank D'Elia remembers: "Along with Ruth came not only the style she'd developed at WMCA, but most of the Good Guys air staff as well! It was great to watch them all interact and almost seamlessly pick up where they left off." Bob Jones began a lengthy career at WNEW and Les Davis became a staple at jazz station WRVR.

D'Elia recalls that Meyer was known for her habit of carrying a can of the soft drink Tab with her at all times, although that can was reputedly often filled with white wine. D'Elia recalls Chuck Renwick finding that out when he started to choke during a meeting, reached for Meyer's Tab and was surprised with a mouthful of wine instead.

A number of country industry groups presented showcases and seminars for the WHN management and staff. The CMA did a day-long seminar on country music. Columbia artists, including Tammy Wynette, George Jones, Freddy Weller and Barbara Fairchild, joined WHN staffers for a luncheon at the Drake Hotel. RCA entertained the station at a luncheon with Dottie West, Danny Davis, Skeeter Davis, Charlie Walker, Johnny Russell and Dickey Lee. Famous Music held a symposium for the station featuring Dot artist Tommy Overstreet. A Country Music

Association board member was quoted in a trade publication that the amount of help "out of Nashville was just astronomical. No one company could have afforded to do the things that the CMA did for WHN."

Of course, country music artists immediately benefitted from having a station playing their music in New York. Charlie Daniels recalls, "Ever since our first hit, I tried to work both sides of the street and put music on our albums for both country and pop radio. When I heard about WHN's switch to country, it was unbelievable. At that time I wasn't even aware of any clubs in New York with country music and now there was a country station in the middle of Manhattan."

Joe Stampley, who had fronted a pop group The Uniques, began recording what was dubbed "country soul" in the early 70s. He says that WHN, "made country music available to millions who had never heard it before. It increased my record sales tremendously."

New York Mayor John V. Lindsay proclaimed March 25th as "Country Music Day" in New York in honor of the station's format change. Bruce Bradley emceed a country music concert that night in Lincoln Center's Philharmonic Hall.

Meyer was approached by Steve Warren, who was working as an associate director for CBS radio sports and doing part time work on air at WPAT-AM/FM. Impressed by his earlier experience working for several country stations, she hired him as music director and weekend air personality.

O'Lunney's, a club on 2nd Avenue and 48th Street in midtown Manhattan that had tried a number of other types of music, switched to a country only entertainment policy. Owner Hugh O'Lunney became a huge country music fan. Former journalist Al Aronowitz, who said he had introduced the Beatles to marijuana at a meeting with Bob Dylan, began booking a "Country In New York" concert series at Madison Square Garden's Felt Forum. Although he booked top artists, including Merle Haggard,

Ed Salamon

Willie Nelson, Dolly Parton and George Jones, his concerts were not successful and he discontinued the series. Aronowitz said that reaction to country artists like Larry Gatlin and Tanya Tucker was overwhelming, but the audiences were always small.

In September, the fledgling HBO carried a concert hosted by Dan Daniel from the Grand Ole Opry to its subscribers in Pennsylvania, New Jersey and New York. The artists included Charlie Rich, Billy "Crash" Craddock, Don Williams and Barbara Fairchild.

There were several major WHN promotions that year. Jack Spector hosted a listener trip to Nashville. WHN held a family picnic at the Queens campus of St. John's University with Bill Anderson performing. Anderson was one of country music's biggest stars at the time. He had a top ten crossover hit with "Still" and a string of recent hits that all placed in the top ten, if not No. 1. Years later, Bill was a great friend to the station and would return time after time to play "guest deejay." Since he had worked as a deejay himself, he was very good at it and at one point considered leaving his music career for a place on the WHN air staff. WHN promoted a Johnny Cash concert at the C.W. Post campus of Long Island University in Nassau County with on-stage appearances by Spector, Bradley, Martin, De Montreux and Daniel, just like the WMCA Good Guys had appeared at that station's concerts.

CHAPTER TWO
1974

"Country Is" – Tom T. Hall (1974)

The Oak Ridge Boys' lead singer Duane Allen recalls, "It was very important to country music to have WHN playing right off the country music charts. It brought country music to the Big Apple, and that, in itself, brought the largest market in the USA into country music. Before the Oak Ridge Boys started singing country, we were singing gospel music. I remember being in New York when I heard WHN blasting out of a record store downtown. Even though the Oaks were not yet in country, the very fact that country was being played in the city was huge for our industry."

Apparently Storer was not satisfied with the station's progress. By early 1974, Jack Kelly had replaced Jack Sullivan as general manager, who brought in a new program director from one of the company's other stations.

John Mazer replaced Ruth Meyer as program director and soon replaced most of the WHN air staff. Mazer came from Storer country station WDEE in Detroit. Before that, Mazer had instituted a country format at WRCP in Philadelphia, so he had experience programming country stations in large urban markets. In the 1960s and early 70s, WRCP was noted for using a stagecoach with staffers dressed as cowboys and cowgirls as a promotional tool.

Dan Daniel left, to be replaced by Larry Kenney in afternoons. Kenney did great impressions of Richard Nixon, Elvis Presley, Paul Lynde, Walter Cronkite, Howard Cosell, Edward Kennedy, David Brinkley, Henry Kissinger, George Patton and Paul Harvey, which he performed for Don Imus' radio show on WNBC. Kenney began his career in radio in 1963, at the age of 15, as a deejay at WIRL, Peoria, Illinois and worked at WOWO, Fort Wayne, Indiana before joining WHN.

Ray Otis was hired for evenings and Del De Montreux moved to overnights, replacing Stan Martin. Otis was once program director of KXOK, a Todd Storz Top 40 station in St. Louis. His big voice and convincing style has made him one of the most utilized voices on radio commercials over the years.

Big Wilson was hired for mornings after leaving WNBC, replacing Jack Spector. Wilson was big; six foot five inches tall and weighed more than 300 pounds. He had the habit of working with his shoes off in the studio. He had previously been a host of the NBC radio network show *Monitor*. Wilson was known for playing piano while on the air and has been compared to Arthur Godfrey. His show was once described as: "It was camp. It was corny. It was addictive." Bruce Bradley left and Jack Spector assumed his shift.

As of August, the station lineup consisted of Big Wilson (mornings), Lee Arnold (middays), Jack Spector (early afternoon), Larry Kenney (afternoon drive), Ray Otis (evenings), Del De Montreux (overnights).

By that time, a trade magazine was trumpeting "A New Rage in New York: Country Music Takes Over." It was a novelty for a fulltime country station to be in America's largest city. In October, *Billboard* magazine's Is Horowitz presented Kelly and Mazer with an award as the publication's Country Station Of The Year.

CHAPTER THREE
1975

"Rhinestone Cowboy" – Glen Campbell (1975)

Despite the changes made during the past two years, Storer was still unhappy with WHN's progress. The company hired a new general manager for the station, Neil Rockoff, and gave him carte blanche to make whatever changes he felt necessary in order to boost ratings and revenues while simultaneously cutting expenses. Rockoff, thirty-eight years old, had come up through the ranks at CBS radio, as manager of CBS Radio Sales and station manager of KNX-FM Los Angeles before becoming GM at Viacom's beautiful music formatted WLAK-FM, Chicago.

As general manager of WLAK, Rockoff was well aware of the success that WMAQ was having programming country music in Chicago. When Rockoff asked WMAQ's general manger, Charlie Warner, for advice, Warner suggested he contact me. Warner and I had met a couple years earlier when he was general manager of WWSW AM & FM in Pittsburgh. At that point, he was trying to decide what to do with his FM station. I suggested that he hire me to program an all oldies format, which had begun to take off in a few cities. Instead, he decided to become Pittsburgh's first FM Top 40 station and compete directly with 13-Q (WKTQ), which was successful with that format on AM. He hired Bob Pittman from WDRQ, Detroit, one of the few people in radio whose stations were doing call-out research to determine listeners' music preferences. Pittman and I would compare notes and that continued when he came to Pittsburgh. Warner was then hired at WMAQ. He called me and told me confidentially that he was planning to change the format of the station to country and how much he admired the sound of WEEP, the station that I was programming in Pittsburgh. He then said, "I have something to ask you." I was expecting him to ask me to be program director of WMAQ, instead he asked if I would show Pittman what I was doing. He said that he would make it up to me someday. I did (although I'm sure Bob could have figured it out for himself), and he did, in less than a year—by introducing Neil Rockoff to me.

Radio and Records had run a full page profile on me in their February 21st issue. At the time, WEEP had the largest audience share of any country station in a top ten market (although country stations in bigger markets had more actual listeners). The station had achieved that by doing a number of things differently. Most country stations at the time were similar to MOR (middle of the road) radio stations in that air personalities were given free rein to talk as much as they wanted. Many had air personalities with hillbilly personas, much like *Hee Haw*. A few stations were a bit more formatted and thought of themselves as modern country radio, but they were still far away from the contemporary hit radio presentation we used at WEEP. Also, like MOR stations, most country stations had a playlist of sixty or more current songs. WEEP, on the other hand, followed the most cutting edge contemporary radio playbook; the station concentrated on a playlist about half the length of others in the format. WEEP's secret weapon was research, which was being done by few stations in any format, least of all by any country station. Pittman and Warner took all those tricks to Chicago, and added a few of their own, like what was considered the most expensive contest in Chicago radio history, "WMAQ's Gonna

Make Me Rich." This was a "don't say hello" contest, in which listeners won prizes if they answered their phones with the station's call letters. It worked well for WMAQ, as the similar "I Listen To The New Sound of 13-Q" had worked for that station in Pittsburgh.

Rockoff visited me in Pittsburgh, listened to WEEP, and asked me to listen to WHN via a telephone listen line. He asked if I could duplicate that sound in New York. WHN sounded no different to me than most country music stations at that time and I knew, based on what had happened in Pittsburgh and Chicago, that a researched format with a short playlist and a contemporary Top 40 presentation could make a real impact quickly. I was so confident that my approach would work, the fact that the station had three program directors in as many years (Alan Hotlen, Ruth Meyer and John Mazer) didn't bother me at all. Neil Rockoff, who called me "The Pittsburgh Kid", had great faith in me and was able to convince Storer to let a twenty-something with less than two years experience as a program director guide the on air sound of their flagship radio station in New York. For WHN to survive, it was important that it attract more listeners in the 25-49 age group, which was the demographic group targeted by most radio advertisers. The conventional thinking among advertisers at the time was that younger listeners had less disposable income and older listeners would not change the brand preferences that they had already developed.

I told Rockoff that I was willing to try to work with all of the existing talent except for morning man, Big Wilson. His presentation was more like the old *Don McNeil Breakfast Club* show than even MOR radio. I couldn't imagine him making the transition to the contemporary approach. Rockoff agreed to make that change, and we reshuffled the air schedule of the remaining air talent. WHN's deejay lineup became Larry Kenny (mornings), Lee Arnold (middays), Jack Spector (early afternoons), Del De Montreux (afternoon drive time), Ray Otis (evenings), and former part-timer Ed Baer (overnights). Former WMCA Good Guy Dean Anthony continued doing weekends.

Radio ratings were estimated by a company that chose a representative panel of listeners and asked them to write down in a daily diary what stations or personalities they listened to. I was really concerned that these diary keepers would not be able to spell Del De Montreux's name well enough so that WHN would get credit for their listening to him. On the other hand, I felt he had been De Montreux for such a long time on WHN, I couldn't ask him to revert to Del Curtis, though I thought long and hard about it. Otherwise the name seemed appropriate for country radio; it sounded Cajun and there were lots of Cajun references in country music at that time.

In June, I arrived in New York and took a cab to Storer House, a brownstone on East 57th Street, which would be my temporary home. Storer also housed company employees from other markets, two to a room, who had business in New York. They would come in the middle of the night from an evening of entertaining clients, invariably waking me up. In the morning the butler, Juan, would ask us, "How do you like your eggs?" and we were sent out with a good breakfast. For my first months I was at WHN, I spent most of my time at the station and only returned to Storer House to sleep.

WHN was located at 400 Park Avenue at the corner of 54th Street in the heart of midtown Manhattan. It would be hard to find a location that would qualify as more opposite from anyone's idea of "country." This area is noted for some of the highest priced real estate in the world and most exclusive neighborhoods. Within blocks were the Waldorf Astoria Hotel and the corporate headquarters for companies including Mercedes Benz, Colgate-Palmolive and Bristol Myers. There was, however, a median between north and southbound traffic that was maintained year round with flowers and greenery.

My move to WHN was front page news in the radio trade

papers. *Radio and Records* put it in a headline in a box in the upper right corner of their front page. *The Tip Sheet*'s front page story called me "one of the most astute programmers and researchers around," and said, "Gotham is about to discover what C & W really is!"

Rockoff had also hired Nick Verbitsky as WHN general sales manager at the same time, from a position as vice president and east coast sales manager of the Christal Company, a radio advertising sales company. In a 1979 interview in *Cash Box*, Verbitsky talked about the market's perception of the station, "In 1973, WHN was not respected by anyone. There was no philosophy, no direction and the station was losing money." Nick and I were both profiled in the August issue of the company's newsletter, *The Storer Story*. Verbitsky had started out as a media estimator at J. Walter Thompson Advertising Agency but entered radio sales as an account executive for the Eastman Company. In 1970, he joined WCBS, where he became the top biller in the station's history before joining Christal. One of Verbitsky's greatest attributes was that he didn't believe that country listeners in New York were any less valuable than the listeners of more mainstream stations. He and his sales staff did not accept any discrimination against the country audience.

As general sales manager, Verbitsky got a corner office with windows. The only other corner office was the general manager's. My program director's office was internal with no windows and adjacent to the music library. The very first day I moved in I got in trouble with the engineer's union. I decided to move the furniture in my office, which included a stereo. One of the engineers noticed and filed a complaint. It seems that any electronic equipment was under their jurisdiction.

WHN had found and was playing perhaps the worst country music album of all time. It was an album of Hank William's recordings overdubbed with a lush string section. The result was music that was equally disliked both by Williams' fans and those who liked more contemporary country music because of the incongruity of the combination. That was the first record to go.

In June, the Robert Altman film *Nashville* debuted. Hailed by critics as a "brilliant mosaic of American life" and a box office hit, the movie won New York Film Critics' Awards for Best Film and Best Director and was nominated for multiple Oscars. Although it did help to create attention for country music, it reinforced some of its negative stereotypes.

Shortly after I arrived at WHN, Rockoff introduced me to Dale Pon, whom he was to hire in August as head of creative services. Dale was part of the team who had launched the ABC-FM stations and had been working at WCBS-FM and WPLJ. Most notably, Pon would later help to create MTV's slogan "I Want My MTV" and much of its marketing. He was passionate about his work and a genius.

To fund the necessary ad campaign we made cuts wherever we could. I actually didn't mind cutting the $100,000 from the programming budget that we were paying per year to Hugh Hellers' company for jingles. At the time, a lot of edgy Top 40 stations were doing without jingles and that was ok by me. As veteran on-air talent were replaced by up and comers, we saved money on payroll as well. We were able to provide Pon with the war chest he needed to make a sufficient ad buy.

Pon recalls receiving encouragement from the Country Music Association. "Jo Walker was the CMA's executive director. She offered to introduce us to Music Row heavyweights and you and I flew with Neil to Music City. I expected Nashville to be a provincial place. And surely didn't expect anyone like the remarkable, effective, open-minded, openhearted, beautiful Jo Walker. She put me at ease right away. Said she had once worked in public relations—and thought it would take great advertising and promotion to overcome the biases against country music in our radio market. I have to come clean. It wasn't anyone in Nashville. It was me. I was the one, guilty of narrow-mindedness. On the way back to New York, I saw that my chance would be to grow myself—and also maybe help others overcome mistaken beliefs."

It was an incredibly difficult task to rebrand and remarket WHN. The station had been country for more than two years during which it had made a number of adjustments to the format. Any New Yorker who might have had any interest in country radio had already seen WHN's previous advertising campaigns and already sampled the station. Nothing makes a bad product fail quicker than advertising. We would have to change the opinions of listeners who had sampled the product and rejected it, which is a lot more challenging than new product introduction. Could we even get potential listeners to try WHN again? WHN had to radically change expectations of what a country radio station in New York could be.

WHN had to make the programming substantially different in order to get the attention of listeners. If country music alone would have been enough to attract a listener, they would already have been listening. WHN had to change enough to make people rethink their opinion of country radio, and that change could not be an incremental one. I really believed that a radical Top 40 style presentation, as well listening to the audience and playing as wide a variety of music that they considered belonged under the country umbrella would make a difference. WHN also would rely on an enthusiastic air staff, who wanted to play music that they really loved, to re-sell the concept of country music radio to New Yorkers. We made changes quickly, though not quickly enough for me.

I confirmed Pam Green, the former programming secretary who had been filling in as music director since the departure of Steve Warren, in that position. Pam was the niece of Nashville music publisher, Tree Music (now SONY) CEO, Jack Stapp, and therefore was country music royalty (Stapp was elected to the Country Music Hall of Fame in 1989). She had great contacts with the Nashville music community.

Ed Salamon

I was also permitted to have an assistant program director. I hired one of the WEEP air staff, Robbie Roman. Robbie had produced the morning talk/music show with Jack Wheeler at WEEP and then hosted the evening show which mixed what was then called "progressive country" music; records by Commander Cody and the Lost Planet Airmen, Marshall Tucker Band, Eagles and other artists with a country sound who were played on FM rock stations but not on country radio, with compatible music from the station's regular playlist. Pam's job was to help pick the music and to interface with the record companies, artists and their management. Robbie's job was to program the music song by song for the WHN air personalities. Music research, which was to evolve into a more important aspect of the station, was initially handled by Pete Kanze. Kanze was a fellow record collector that I knew and was willing to take an entry level position to be a part of WHN.

WHN did not overtly promote itself as a country music station. Unfortunately, many New Yorkers had a negative perception of country music. We knew if we could get New Yorkers to listen to WHN, they would like it, but the label "country" was a barrier. We did know that potential listeners liked country artists like Johnny Cash, Kenny Rogers, Dolly Parton, Linda Ronstadt, Anne Murray and others, and they became the focus of WHN's promotion. The station's slogan became "WHN gives you music you wana hear." I remember that Pon's first suggestion was "Booze, broads and bad times," but maybe he meant that as a joke.

The most transparent way to market the concept of a listener programmed radio station was to promote request lines. Promoting a methodology of call-out research would not have been as easy. WHN already had a request line, 212-688-6752. Even though our budget was tight, we decided to buy 688-1050 from Ostreicher Realty, who had the number, so that WHN's 1050 dial position would be mentioned every time the request line was promoted on the air.

Kanze recalls that early in the request line a local artist had friends and family flood the request lines with calls for his amateurish recording titled "Tracy Lee." Since we seldom received so many calls for such an obscure record, we examined the data more closely. Even though the calls turned out to be from only a few people calling repeatedly, Storer's lawyers ordered that WHN play the record once and let the artist know that time in advance.

Jack Spector would not take direction. He was a New York radio legend, but I thought his presentation was a throwback to the 60s. Jack would not stop using rhyming couplets (his sign off was "look out street, here come my feet"), calling himself "The Kosher Cowboy From Coney Island" or giving sports scores to insignificant games. Actually, the other former WMCA deejays had characteristic sign-offs as well. Ed Baer's was "Let's have lunch sometime" and Dan Daniel's was "I love you . . . and especially you, size nine," a reference to his wife, Rose Mary. As a veteran talent, Spector was also expensive. We decided to replace him when his contract expired. Jack went on to a long run at WCBS-FM, where he sounded great playing the oldies. He also worked at WNBC, WPIX and finally at WHLI in Long Island where he passed away in 1984 while on the air.

I conducted a search, listened to hundreds of tapes, and had several suggestions, but John Mazer, who was still at WHN, having been promoted to operations manager, was emphatic that we hire an experienced New York talent. He was so dismissive of my suggestions to bring in someone from another market that he persuaded Rockoff to his way of thinking. Of the available New Yorkers, I chose Bob Wayne as the best of the lot. I should point out that this is the only time that I can remember being overruled by Rockoff. I had quickly gained Rockoff's confidence and my programming decisions, as different as they were from other country stations, were normally unquestioned.

Bob "The Wizard" Wayne has been called "the essence of

hip New York style." He was a former air talent at Top 40 stations KDWB, KCBQ, WSAI and WUBE, who had most recently worked at WCBS-FM. He had a great understanding of brevity of content and I thought his soft delivery would work well in middays and slotted him between Lee Arnold and Del De Montreux. On his first day, Wayne quipped while announcing a song, "Freddy Fender—I knew his brother Ronnie Running-board." He soon came to an understanding that neither the artists nor their music were to be objects of humor.

WHN's advertisers were another likely target of air personalities' humor. Tom Carvel was a Greek businessman who voiced the commercials for his Carvel ice cream stores in a distinctive raspy voice which invited imitation. Carvel didn't mind an occasional joke at his own expense, but was adamant that no one make fun of his products. This was not easy to avoid, as they included the ice cream novelties "Cookie Puss" and "Fudgie The Whale."

I soon learned that minimum AFTRA scale at WHN was about $40,000 a year. This meant that even WHN's overnight air personality made nearly twice as much as I did. Rockoff soon gave me perks that I hadn't negotiated for, including a company car and a parking space. However, for a long time I was paid less than any of the full time air talent. I'm sure they knew that, which made it more challenging to win their confidence.

News director Mike Prelee's contract was up and, like Jack Spector, he was considerably over union scale. WHN didn't renew him and promoted Charlie Kaye to news director. Kaye recalls, "In the days before radio was deregulated, virtually all major market music stations on the AM band, such as WHN, had 24-hour news departments, and WHN had a fine one. We talked about the folks who passed through that newsroom. They included some of the first women news anchors in New York radio, Rita Sands and Kate Doordan, and one of the first African-American radio news anchors, Ann Tripp. Among the other people at WHN News during that era were Mike Prelee, Jim Gordon, Gene Ladd, Marvin Scott, Steve Powers, Ian MacLeod and Joe Bragg."

Kaye helped move the station away from an MOR radio news approach toward a more contemporary sound. Charlie took his role as news director very seriously. We soon clashed. Without advising me, Kaye had broken in to regular programming with a lengthy tornado warning. I tuned in WHN to hear Kaye speaking from "the tornado desk" advising people "if you are in your car, get into a ditch." At the time, I thought we were interrupting music to make a big thing out of nothing. WHN moved the news from the top of the hour to ten minutes before, so we could be out by five minutes to the hour, when WABC went into news. WHN could then be playing music while most music stations were in news. This was also designed to take advantage of the rating service's methodology which awarded an entire quarter hour of listening for five continuous minutes within the hour. If a WABC listener punched into WHN when WABC went into news, our intention was to keep them for a ten minute music sweep and get credit for two quarter hours of listening. We would always announce the time at the beginning of the music sweep as :55 and the end of the sweep as :05. WHN air personalities would never give the time as 6:20, 7:10, 9:30, 10:10 or 11:30, as they were the frequencies of AM competitors WVNJ, WOR, WPAT, WINS and WNEW.

WHN also initiated the "soft" transition to news to minimize its impact as an interruption. Rather than a sounder, news now began with a conversation initiated by the deejay with the newsman that morphed into a newscast. Transitioning to news, Larry Kenney might say something like, "Gene Ladd's here. Gene, what's new with that fire up in the Bronx." Gene might reply, "Well, Larry, at this point there are no reported injuries . . ." and continue right through the newscast. It added to the deejays responsibilities because they had to be aware and sound interested in the news. Ladd recalls, "Reporter Joe Bragg broke the color barrier at City Hall for broadcast journalism. It was one very good radio station top to bottom and I am proud to have been part of it."

Another unusual detail of WHN was the programming of commercials. Maureen Lesourd and Carol McGuire in the commercial traffic department became proficient at scheduling commercials in a strict order. Any commercials read live by the deejay were to be scheduled at either the beginning or end of a commercial "stop set." The pre-recorded commercials were arranged with all the thirty second spots first, followed by the sixty second spots. Within those categories, those with the highest production values (music or sound effects) would be scheduled last. No more than one commercial for a type of client was permitted within a stop set. I believed that this was the best way to hold listeners' interest through the commercials.

WHN also began to promote its weather forecasts as "radar weather." Actually, most stations took their forecasts from the same National Weather Service predictions which utilized radar. WHN's use of that term made the station sound more high tech than its competitors.

About the time I arrived at WHN, a record was released that became the anthem of the station. "Rhinestone Cowboy" had been written and released the previous year by New Yorker Larry Weiss. The song described his dreams of being a star while walking the streets of Manhattan. Glen Campbell, a household name because of his long running television show, *The Glen Campbell Goodtime Hour,* had just released his version. WHN jumped on the song and it ultimately reached the top of both the country and pop charts. That song galvanized the feelings of the station and its listeners of survival and making it, particularly when the chips are down.

"Thank God I'm A Country Boy" by John Denver was also on the charts that year. It was a million seller and a huge hit both on the pop and country charts. It was a very positive affirmation for country radio listeners. Denver had been considered a pop artist and his early records, like "Take Me Home Country Roads," were hardly played on country radio, though they were big pop hits. By 1975, he and his music became solidly a part of the country format, a reverse from the usual country to pop crossover.

I met WHN's evening air personality, Ray Otis, on my first day in New York. Neil Rockoff was walking me around the station so that I would have my bearings when I started work the next morning. When we walked into the studio, Ray had his feet up on the console and was looking at a television set, with the sound of the station turned down. Neil seemed embarrassed. I wondered if I would be able to coach Ray effectively. In my mind air talent should be always be as engaged as if they are flying a 747.

In order to attract the largest possible audience, we had to cover as much country music territory as possible. Bill Gavin who had a trade publication, *The Gavin Report*, was a friend and mentor and he had convinced me that variety was the key to successful radio programming. The core of the playlist was the biggest country hits, but WHN also wanted to be on the cutting edge with records that would become the next big hits. We believed if listeners would hear a new record on WHN before they heard it on another station, they would think that the station was playing WHN's music. The station's mix was about half current and half non-current. Those "oldies" would range from songs that had just gone off the charts and were still played frequently, "recurrents," to those country hits that went back as far as a couple decades, with special emphasis on records that had been successful on both the country and pop charts. There were more than 2,000 songs in regular rotation at WHN.

Some records in WHN's oldies rotation had not been country hits, but were by artists now played on country radio. Del

Ed Salamon

De Montreux had a problem with one of these songs, "One Hell Of A Woman" by Mac Davis. Del would not say the word "hell." I argued with him about it, and he finally relented. When I had more experience as a program director, I would regret doing that. In fact, I would have used his refusal to say "hell" as a something to talk about on the air. However, in 1975, I was inflexible about the station's formatics, insisting on consistency to a fault.

In evenings, I wanted to replicate the "progressive country" show we did in Pittsburgh. I ultimately decided that the best host for that would be Jessie, so she replaced Ray Otis. Ray continued to work in New York radio, notably for WNEW. I later hired him as host for "The Great Sounds," a nationally syndicated show featuring the artists of the 40s and 50s.

Jessie was originally from the New York area, but I first encountered her when she was hired as the first female air talent on WDVE, the ABC network's progressive rock station in Pittsburgh. Jessie was the air name she had used on the radio since college. She did not use a last name professionally. At this time, female air personalities were still a novelty and often attracted unwanted attention from listeners who felt they shared a connection. She then worked at the market's major Top 40 station, 13-Q, making her also the first female Top 40 deejay in the market. Like many personalities on those stations, Jessie had a real passion to share music she loved with listeners. The music she loved included progressive country. By this time, John Mazer had left the station and there were objections to hiring someone without New York radio experience. The novelty of having a female air personality on New York AM radio, at that time still the dominant band, didn't hurt. Jessie soon was featured in a personality profiles in the Sunday News, the Village Voice and elsewhere. Jessie was typical of the air talent I would hire for WHN; she had a firm grasp on the formatics of Top 40 radio and was able to bring the element of personality within that structure.

Like Lee Arnold, she had a true enthusiasm for the music that came across to listeners.

Jim Duncan, then country editor for *Radio and Records*, recalls, "WHN had great on-air personalities who were great communicators and didn't try to sound country. The station was very much a part of the community. It showed listeners that it was cool to like country music. They presented concerts and events that made people realize that country music wasn't just for people from Tennessee, Kentucky, Texas, Oklahoma or Alabama."

WHN soon got in trouble with Storer's legal department over the new morning show with Larry Kenney. Among the character voices that Kenney did was a fictional cab driver named Sid. Sid would do funny bits with Kenney and a recurring topic would often entail Sid being stuck in traffic. A Storer executive visiting New York was listening to the station one day and advised us that we could no longer have Sid talking about traffic because that would constitute a false traffic report for anyone who did not get the joke.

In retrospect, I'm surprised that the conservative Storer lawyers never expressed concern about the lyric content of some of the "progressive country" songs that played during Jessie's show. In 1971, the Federal Communications Commission (FCC) had reminded radio stations that broadcast material "promoting" or "glorifying" the use of drugs could endanger station licenses. WHN played songs like "Willin'" by Linda Ronstadt ("give me weed, whites and wine"), "Wildwood Weed" by Jim Stafford ("Smokin' them wildwood flowers got to be a habit, take a trip and never leave the farm") and "Casey Jones" by the Grateful Dead ("Drivin' that train, high on cocaine"). I felt comfortable playing them because I believed that those songs show the negative affects of drug usage and because they were also being played by FM rock stations, including WNEW-FM, in the market. Luckily the FCC had no such concern about the misuse of alcohol, as songs about drunkenness were a common theme in country music at the time.

Dale Pon and I collaborated on an ad campaign consisting of Dale's slogan "There's a whole lot of good in this country" on ads featuring the biggest stars playing on WHN. It was critical that Dale and I have the same vision for the station; the promotion had to match the on-air sound and vice versa. This common vision was not always easily arrived at, and I remember a fist fight or two with him in those less politically correct times. Johnny Cash, Glen Campbell, Linda Ronstadt and Anne Murray, among others, agreed to let WHN use their name and likeness to promote the station at no cost. In a 1979 *Cash Box* interview, Pon said, "Any artist we have ever asked to come and help us out has done so and none of them have ever asked to be paid." Later, Anne Murray told me she may have regretted her decision: "Before I was on the WHN ad campaign, I was able to walk around New York anonymously. Now everybody knows who I am and stops me in Bloomingdale's." Murray's comment recalls a story about Loretta Lynn repeated around WHN. Lynn was walking near Central Park and was approached by a couple who wanted a photo. Lynn posed obligingly, but then she was handed the camera. The couple had wanted her to take a photo of them. Country artists had been that anonymous in New York prior to WHN's success.

WHN posters appeared in subways and complementary television ads were bought with money we had saved by cutting items from the station's budget. It was key to have the on air sound reflect the ads, so we put music by the artists featured in the ads in high rotation. Those artists featured in our ads became WHN's superstars, so we were very fortunate to have the participation of all of the true giants of country music.

Not only did the music on WHN match the "There's a whole lot of good in this country" slogan of the ads, but so did the contesting. Listeners were asked to call in and give an example of something that was good about the country in order to receive a prize, determined at random from a tape cartridge on which prize descriptions were recorded.

The television ads were simple and effective. The artist would talk about their music and then say "Ten-fifty, WHN." It was a soft sell, but an endorsement of the station by some of the biggest artists of popular music who were played by many New York stations at the time. Dale Pon, who directed the television commercials, remembers, "Anne Murray was warm, unaffected and as friendly as a person could be. Crystal Gayle is an accomplished performer, but it was her shy laughter that was the most dazzling. Freddy Fender talked about his songs and the 'importance of a good back beat.'" Pon was particularly impressed by Johnny Cash: "Johnny Cash always put all of himself into everything he did. He certainly did that when he went in front of a movie camera for us. He and I did a little Q&A to get into particular topics. And it was so important to Mr. Cash to be totally honest in his answers that, walking away from the film lights, he was spent. His strength and wholehearted effort made an indelible mark on me. Since then, I feel like a bum when I'm not tired at the end of the day."

In a later campaign, Pon created subway posters with the station slogan in Spanish and had them posted in high density Hispanic areas. This was probably the first time that any country station advertised in Spanish. Subway posters of Charley Pride also helped the perception of the diversity of the artists played on WHN. Pon suggested a contest where listeners would call in and talk about "the music you wanna hear." The varied accents from Brooklyn, Queens, New Jersey, as well as the ethnic accents, let listeners know that their friends and neighbors listened to WHN, helping to dispel the feeling that country music was somehow alien to New York City. The key to attracting black and Hispanic listeners to country radio proved to be pretty simple: invite them. Of course we made sure that once they tuned in they heard voices of people who sounded just like them and, of course, lots of music by the artists featured in the advertizing, Charley Pride and Freddy Fender. While other country stations followed WHN in playing records and instituting the structured air personality formatics, at the time, I did not notice any other country stations that specifically reached out to black and Hispanic listeners.

Editor Patrick Carr would later write in *Country Music* magazine: "Imagine you're in New York . . . you're taking a cab ride down Broadway, which is international city, and the black cab driver has 'The Pill' on the radio. Then you're eating pasta and the waiters are crooning along with Glen Campbell. Then you go to a Chinese laundry, the Puerto Rican deli, the Port Authority bus terminal, and you get John Denver back-to-back with the Eagles, Willie Nelson, Hank Snow, Freddy Fender, Dolly Parton . . . all of which is very interesting. . . . WHN has not only succeeded in New York, but has managed to cater to the musical vacuum of the inner city—that phrase, now ominous with racism and class prejudice, which really means a non-white dominated population—almost as well as it has (naturally enough) penetrated the suburbs and the white working class fringes."

That fall there was a cocktail party with the WHN talent and management for the Storer directors at Storer House. We were able to get Johnny Cash to make an appearance and shake hands. By virtue of his television show, which ran on the ABC network from 1969 through 1981, Cash was probably the most recognizable country star and the icon of the format at the time. After the meeting, Neil and I were called aside and told that we had six months to turn WHN around, or Storer was going in a different direction with the station. We felt we were on the right track, but the summer rating book had actually been down. When you change a radio station, the first people to know about it are the current listeners who, presumably, already liked what they were hearing. The ad campaign was just then airing and we hoped it would bring enough new listeners in the fall ratings to keep WHN country.

The Eagles first hit the national country charts with "Lyin' Eyes" in October of that year. But WHN had played their Top 40 hits "Take It Easy," "Peaceful Easy Feeling," "Already Gone" and "Best Of My Love" in oldies rotation since I arrived. I can't believe that country radio was so slow to embrace this act, but I don't think they had been initially promoted by the label to the format. A few years later a lot of the records produced in Nashville would have harmonies and arrangements very similar to the Eagles. Elektra's local promotion man was Bruce Shindler. He always made sure Pam and I were aware of any music that might possibly fit on the station. As a result, many records that were not intended as country releases by the label were played on WHN and, when successful, caught on with the format nationally.

In fact, many of the records we played at WHN were not intended as country releases, but were called to our attention by the local promotion men in the market who were interested in getting airplay for any of the records on their label. Capitol's Joe Maimone was from the old school; he dressed up as Santa Claus when he visited us at Christmastime that year. Ray Free of Epic records greeted everyone with "ool-ya-koo," a bebop slang term made famous by jazzman Dizzy Gillespie. Matty Matthews, the local Columbia promotion man, also had a catch phrase; "doin' it all." RCA's Dave Morrell was a record collector and Beatles fan. Ray D'Ariano and later Sammy Vargas, one of the first Latinos at a major label, and Barry Goodman handled local promotion for MCA. Mickey Wallach was the local ABC promotion representative. They generally visited WHN weekly and often escorted their label's artists to the station.

I always felt that it was important to have a novelty record on the playlist during rating periods to create word of mouth conversation about WHN. When there wasn't a current record that fit that description, I would find an older record and revive it, playing it in rotation as a current single. For the fall rating period of 1976, WHN revived "Phantom 309" by Red Sovine, which had been a country hit in 1967. It was re-released by Gusto records and charted in the middle of the national country charts that year as other stations added it. This was only the first of the records that had a second run on the charts because of WHN airplay.

Instead of having visiting artists be interviewed by the air talent, as was the usual practice in radio stations, I had them sit in as "guest deejays." I felt that listeners might tune out if an artist that was not one of their favorites was being interviewed, because that portion of the show would be all about a single artist. When an artist was guest deejay, they followed the format, playing other artists records, giving time, traffic and weather reports and even reading commercials. The novelty of this seemed to keep all listeners engaged. I had thought of this at WEEP when Jimmy Dean was being interviewed by the afternoon air personality, Gary Semro. Dean had crossover hits with "Big Bad John" and "P.T. 109" in the early 60s, and would later become better known for his line of pork sausage. Generally, meeting artists is a positive experience. Dean proved to be the exception to this rule. He was rude and demeaning to everyone at the station. Coming out of a commercial break, Dean mocked Semro on the air, asking him why he spoke in one voice while off air and used a different "radio" voice when the microphone was on. I decided that I would never put one of my air talents in a position where they could be ridiculed by a visiting artist, and the guest deejay concept was the result. Dean's comment certainly didn't hurt Semro's career; he won *Billboard* magazine's award as 1974 Major Market Country Air Personality of the Year and later worked at WCBS-FM in New York (as Gary Clark). In 1976, Dean released a narration thanking his mother, "I.O.U." Although one would think this was just the kind of novelty record that would have done well at WHN, we didn't play it. Unfortunately the song was more than six minutes long, about twice as long as an average record at the time and we didn't think it was worth the two spots on the format clock. Nevertheless, the single reached top ten in the country charts and sold over a million copies without any airplay on WHN.

Pam Green recalls that Charley Pride was the first artist to be a WHN guest deejay on August 8th. Another of the early guest deejays on WHN was Johnny Cash. *Radio and Records* ran a photo of me directing Cash in the studio that day. Cash was a good friend of WHN and frequent visitor to the radio station. He had an apartment at 40 Central Park South during the 1970s. His ABC television series *The Johnny Cash Show* had featured artists including Bob Dylan, Neil Young and Gordon Lightfoot, just as we did on WHN.

Charlie Daniels, like most of the artists, liked the idea of being a guest deejay rather than the standard interview format. Daniels says, "It gave listeners a chance to get to know us beyond our music. It was always a pleasure."

C. W. McCall sat in as a guest deejay on November 20th. He premiered his single "Convoy," which would eventually reach No. 1 on both the country and pop charts and sell more than a million copies. C.W. McCall, a pseudonym for Colorado advertising executive Bill Fries, sparked an interest in citizens band radios with that hit, and many country songs began to incorporate CB slang into their lyrics.

At that time, CB and truck songs became to country radio what surfing songs had been to pop music in the 60s. The truck themed hits included Merle Haggard's "Movin' On," Joe Stampley's "Roll On Big Mama," and Cledus Maggard and The Citizen's Band had "The White Knight." In addition to "Phantom 309," Sovine would have the CB themed hit, "Teddy Bear," a song about a handicapped kid who talked to truckers on the CB radio. WHN printed a CB dictionary and offered it to listeners who sent in a stamped, self-addressed envelope. Demand was so high we had to reprint the piece several times.

Ronnie Milsap was another frequent guest deejay on WHN. When he had done that on WEEP, I had all of the promos and live commercials translated into Braille so this blind artist could do everything any other guest deejay did. We continued that practice at WHN. Milsap probably had more No. 1 national country hits than any artist during WHN's glory days, and in 1977 we were glad that the New York single sales of his "It Was Almost Like A Song" to WHN listeners would help convince WABC to add the record, finally giving Ronnie the crossover hit that he deserved.

Michael Martin Murphey had two big WHN hits that year "Wildfire" and "Carolina In The Pines," neither of them made the national country charts, but they were both pop hits. In 1982, Michael would sign with Liberty records, who marketed his releases to country radio, where he had a string of national country hits, one of which "What's Forever For" crossed over onto the pop charts. Murphey's style hadn't changed all that much, just the way he was promoted by his record label. Pam Green and I once went to see him perform at the Rainbow Grill. There was a group of foreigners who kept talking loudly during his set. Murphey asked them to quiet down so the rest of the audience could hear his lyrics. Their interpreter responded that their lack of attention was because they weren't from this country and didn't speak English. Murphey responded that they were apparently from a country where rudeness was acceptable.

Dolly Parton was a guest deejay on WHN on November 26th, the day before she and Freddy Fender appeared in the Macy's Thanksgiving Day Parade. Fender's "Before The Next Teardrop Falls" and "Wasted Days and Wasted Nights" had both been million selling singles that year. Parton was yet to have a crossover hit, but several of her songs, including "I Will Always Love You" had topped the country charts. Dale Pon recalls speaking with Dolly that day: "I met her briefly just before airtime. New

York City was in terrible financial shape. In October, the well-known *Daily News* headline read '(President) Ford To City: Drop Dead.' I asked Ms. Parton if she thought we New Yorkers would get through the tough times ahead. She said, 'Of course you will. It'll hurt, but you'll keep trying.' Over the years, her remarks have steadied me."

Alan Colmes, today best known as for his talk shows on Fox radio and television and previously with *Hannity and Colmes*, was another part time air personality. Colmes remembers, "The biggest thing about WHN for me was it was the first time anyone put me on the radio in my hometown of New York, the No. 1 radio market. In August of 1975 I'd just been fired as morning man at WEZE in Boston when the station went to a religious format, and my old boss, Carl Grande, rehired me at WNHC in New Haven, not too far from the Big Apple. But the icing on the cake was having the opportunity to have my name and voice on a New York radio station, even if it was on weekends, and even if I wasn't able to do more than introduce or back announce records. I finally made it to New York! General manager Neil Rockoff, and general sales manager Nick Verbitsky (who later became the general manager) were smart managers who supported program director Ed Salamon's very prescient move to introduce the mechanics of Top 40 radio to the country format, aided by music director Pam Green. And they were willing to spend the money to blanket the city with big promotional campaigns to give the station the kind of footprint you need in New York, aided by the tremendous marketing skills of Dale Pon. It was a great team and I was thrilled to be even a small part of it."

The fall ratings were released on December 16th. Neil Rockoff sent a congratulatory memo informing the staff that WHN was now No. 2 in New York (second only to WABC) among adults 25-49 and "the second biggest radio station in the entire world," noting that it was a complete team effort that did it. Neil also said, "the best is yet to come" and he was right.

Ed Salamon

WHN ran ads saying, "WHN, the biggest thing since rock 'n' roll: No. 2 Adults 25-49 all week long." The ads compared our position among the listeners desired by national advertisers to Top 40 WABC, which played rock and roll, to which we were a distant, but competitive second. By virtue of New York being America's largest radio market, it meant that we also had far more listeners per average quarter hour than any other country radio station had attracted in history.

CHAPTER FOUR
1976

"New Kid in Town" – Eagles (1976)

On January 2nd, WHN started a "Tell Us Something Good That Happened To You Lately" contest. All of our contests were designed to get a mix of listeners' voices on the air. When listeners heard people with accents like themselves phoning in, they didn't feel that country music was foreign to New York. Rather than give away large fantasy prizes like vacations, cars or large amounts of money, we tried to reflect the realities of WHN listeners' lives. Besides, WHN didn't have a large budget for prizes. The contest offered, "We'll help you make it through the week with rent, groceries, steak and jeans. We may even pay your telephone bill." I think the jeans may have been a trade with a sponsor and the rest were cash prizes. We just suggested how the cash could be used to make the prize more relatable.

For the winter rating period, WHN revived "Deck of Cards," the 1959 hit narration by Wink Martindale. The record was a remake of a 1948 country hit about a soldier who used his deck of cards as a Bible. "Deck of Cards" became the No. 2 record at WHN and, after it was re-released by ABC/Dot records, reportedly sold 13,000 copies in the New York market which *Cash Box* reported as, "an incredible achievement for any country record."

Although WHN didn't use jingles, we did begin using custom

production for contests done at TM Enterprises, the premiere radio jingle producer at the time. One day Neil Rockoff called and asked me to come into his office. Meeting with Rockoff was Jim West, a representative of TM whose pitches I had been politely resisting for several months. "This man says we have no musical identity," said Rockoff, looking concerned. I'm still not sure whether Rockoff knew exactly what West meant by that at the time, but West was telling Rockoff that we had no jingles. I explained my position on jingles, but ultimately I agreed that WHN could benefit from some production work at TM. Unlike other TM clients, WHN did not agree to pay royalties on their production, on the basis that Dale Pon and I went to TM's Dallas studios to help write and direct each session. At TM we used the big voice of Brice Armstrong for imaging. Armstrong later became a renowned voice actor for animation. Rockoff (as executive producer), Pon and I won prestigious CLIO advertising award certificates for two different campaigns we wrote and produced at TM.

The January 17th edition of *Record World* carried a cover story about WHN that said, "The rating success of WHN (New York) in the closing months of 1975 has convinced supporters of the station and of country music that WHN, three years after its format change, has become the showcase for country music in the nation's largest market that has been lacking for so long. In the October-November rating sweeps, the Storer Broadcasting property has risen to second in the market among adults aged 25-49 in average quarter hour totals. A year ago those same sweeps placed WHN fourteenth." The headlines read "Fourteenth to Second," "Rockoff's Turnaround," and "New Country Concepts."

One of the most popular and improbable WHN hits of the year was "Paloma Blanca" by a Dutch group, the George Baker Selection. They had had a top twenty pop hit several years earlier with "Little Green Bag." I can't explain what was country about the record, but not only did the WHN audience love it, it ultimately placed in the thirties on the national country charts as other country stations picked it up. Slim Whitman recorded a version especially for the country market, but it did not chart.

"Queen Of The Silver Dollar" by Dave and Sugar was a bigger hit on WHN than nationally. The original version by Doyle Holly had been a much requested song at WEEP, so this new version was an early add at WHN. The trio had been back up singers for Charley Pride and had a consistent string of top ten hits, including No. 1 hits "The Door Is Always Open," "Tear Time" and "Golden Tears"; great records which unfortunately are not played by country radio anymore.

In February, the Lone Star Café opened in a former Schrafft's restaurant on 5th Avenue and 13th Street. Two executives at the Wells, Rich, Greene advertising agency, Mort Cooperman and Bill McGivney, had approached WHN for a promotional relationship for their idea of a Manhattan restaurant featuring national country music acts. The club was recognizable for many blocks because of the 40 foot sculpture of an iguana, created by Bob "Daddy-o" Wade, on the roof of the building. I always wondered what the ladies who lunched at Schrafft's thought when they showed up and found The Lone Star Café instead.

Before The Lone Star, only O'Lunney's had occasionally booked national acts in Manhattan. I had my first meeting with Crystal Gayle and her husband/manager Bill Gatzimos there. Bill recalls that Crystal played O'Lunney's with local musicians backing her before she had a band of her own. Although she is Loretta Lynn's sister, Crystal had a different style which later allowed her records to cross onto the pop charts. The only other New York area venue to feature national country acts on a regular basis was the Blue Ribbon Inn in Hillside, New Jersey. Its owner, Freddie Wenzler, known as "Freddie the German Cowboy," would act as master of ceremonies dressed in western garb, announcing the acts in his German accent.

Hilly Kristal, a huge country fan and the owner of the club

Ed Salamon

CBGB at 315 Bowery at Bleecker Street in Manhattan, had been discussing a similar idea with us. The club's initials were originally intended to stand for Country Bluegrass Blues, but it embraced the new wave and later punk rock movements instead. We stayed in touch and he would put my name on the club's guest list whenever I asked. I didn't go as often as I wish I had. The club was located in a rough section of town populated with drug addicts, alcoholics, panhandlers and homeless. Nevertheless, I recall seeing Blondie, the Tuff Darts and The Ramones, who played at CBGB often and were my favorites among the bands that I saw there.

"The Lone Star Café has admittedly had a helping hand from a powerful radio station, today one of the largest in the United States . . . WHN 1050," wrote the *Swissair Gazette* a couple years later. I knew that the acts we played on WHN would appreciate The Lone Star Café as a more convenient venue as a showcase for press. Bill Dick replaced McGivney as Mort's partner, and I helped them make the necessary contacts. At that time FM rock stations, including New York's WNEW and WLIR, were doing live concert broadcasts and I thought a country radio station should, too. WHN broadcast live from the Lonestar Café once or twice a week, depending on their bookings. Generally, we would air the 10:00 pm set live. Sometimes, if it was not a core WHN act, we would air the live show at midnight. The consistent promotion of upcoming broadcasts gave the Lone Star Café exposure that would have been unaffordable, and the club gave WHN a physical link with its listeners and a great place to entertain clients. The club had a narrow interior. There was not room for many people between the bar on the left and the stage on the right. Much of the audience sat to the left of the stage and craned their neck to see the show. To the left of the stage was also a staircase wound to the upstairs, where the only good view of the stage was from the tables along the railing.

One of WHN's earliest live broadcasts from the Lone Star

Café was with Mickey Gilley. That's when I found out about the call and response audience participation routine to "Cotton-Eyed Joe" which was not appropriate for broadcast. The Federal Communication Commission did not tolerate any indecent or obscene language on radio. Unbeknownst to us at WHN, it had become a tradition that audiences responded to this song's lyrics with the barn yard term "bullshit," mimicking the act of kicking off barnyard muck. At first I couldn't understand what the crowd was saying. Then it dawned on me. WHN received no complaints, so I assume the audience was inaudible over the air. I had a ten second delay installed before the next live broadcast. Two years later, in a landmark case, the US Supreme Court would uphold the FCC against New York radio station WBAI, which broadcast a version of George Carlin's routine "Seven Words You Can Never Say On Television," which contained that same word. WHN could well have suffered the same fate based on the Gilley's broadcast.

"The Winner" by Bobby Bare was also a much bigger hit on WHN than it was nationally. Bobby often performed at the Lone Star Café and Shel Silverstein (the writer of that song, "A Boy Named Sue," "Sylvia's Mother" and many others) sometimes attended. I really enjoyed hanging out with him and Bobby. Silverstein's talents seemed endless; he wrote best-selling children's books and drew cartoons for *Playboy*, as well as writing hit songs. Bobby's career extended back to the rock and roll novelty song "All American Boy," which had been released under the name of Bare's friend Bill Parsons while Bare was in the Army. Bare recorded hits like "Shame On Me," "500 Miles," and "Detroit City," which were just as big on the pop as the country charts during the folk era. WHN played them all in the "oldies" rotation. Another of Silverstein's songs recorded by Bobby Bare, "Rosalie's Good Eats Café," though not a single, had been played in the overnight hours on WHN and became a listener favorite.

Ed Salamon

The Lone Star clientele often included artists. One afternoon, Pam Green and I were having lunch there and I noticed a scruffy looking patron sitting alone at a nearby table. I thought he looked like singer-songwriter Tom Waits. I asked Pam if she would go over and find out, and indeed that's who it was. Waits had received critical acclaim for his own records and had written "Ol' 55," which was recorded by the Eagles and played on WHN. It seems that Waits listened to WHN whenever he was in New York and had recorded his own version of the country hit "Phantom 309" the previous year on his album, *Nighthawks at the Diner*. We asked Waits to join us, but he said he preferred to drink alone.

Hee Haw regular, *Playboy* Playmate and then Hugh Hefner girlfriend Barbie Benton sat in as guest deejay with Del De Montreux assisting on February 9th. She had a hit with "Brass Buckles" on the *Playboy* label the previous year. I'm sure by the time she arrived at WHN, some of the *Playboy* magazines with her nude photo layouts had circulated around the station. A photo from that day shows Del looking like he was wowed by her presence.

The notion of a female country music deejay was still so novel that many in the industry who had not heard Jessie assumed she was a male. A number of WHN staff attended the Country Radio Seminar in Nashville this year, and when we arrived at the hotel, we found that Jessie and I were assigned to share a room as part of the CRS "buddy system." The hotel staff scrambled and made other accommodations. As country stations became aware of Jessie's success at WHN, many would hire a woman for the evening time slot.

The April issue *Country Music* magazine ran an article by Mary Sue Price, "Can New York Take The Real Thing," which contained many inaccuracies and criticized WHN for what she considered "no attempt to bring out the historical roots of country music." The May issue contained a retraction by the magazine's editor, Patrick Carr; ". . . writer Mary Sue Price managed to convey the impression that WHN-AM, the third largest radio station in the USA, had failed in its effort to market country music on the streets of New York. Fortunately for the now-furious WHN, and unfortunately for *Country Music* (which now must own up to the egg on its face), such is not the case." Carr went on to say, ". . . WHN has actually realized the Impossible Dream (long dreamed by the CMA and other boosters) that country music, sufficiently adapted, could be the biggest thing since the can opener with people who really aren't country at all. It is certainly, by far, the biggest country station in the world." Carr explained how the success of a country station in New York had helped Madison Avenue advertising agencies warm to buying country radio and quoted Neil Rockoff exclaiming, "We should get bouquets from WWVA."

In 1976, Marty Robbins re-signed with Columbia records after several years with MCA. His first single was "El Paso City," a sequel to his 1959 hit "El Paso," which was a perennial favorite WHN oldie. Robbins sat in as guest deejay during Bob Wayne's shift. Afterwards, Columbia promotion manager Matty Matthews took me to lunch with Marty at a restaurant near Rockefeller Center. When lunch was over, I offered to get a cab for Marty, and escort him back to his hotel. When he got in, the cab driver asked Marty where he was staying. It was the Hilton, only a half block away.

Despite WHN's success, Neil Rockoff looked for ways to cut operating expenses. One day, after receiving a bill from one of the performing rights societies which collect payments for writers and publishers, he sent me a note saying that I had to choose either BMI or ASCAP. The third, SESAC, was far less expensive. Pam Green and I did an analysis of the music WHN played that convinced him we needed to keep both. It would have been hard to work with half of the music on the charts.

Neil Rockoff was a fan of the designer Gucci. He always wore Gucci loafers and a Gucci belt buckle. He suggested that his executives do the same. At the time, I was more likely to dress in jeans and one of the many tee shirts given to me to promote a new artist or album. At Rockoff's urging, Robbie Roman, Dale Pon and I went to Gucci's store to buy ourselves Gucci loafers. It was a very upscale store, similar to Tiffany or Cartier. The salespeople were formal with us to the point of being condescending. Although I have a narrow foot, I found a pair of loafers that I could wear. As I recall, Dale wasn't lucky enough to find a pair that fit and we kidded him about not being Cinderella. Robbie must have dressed particularly casual that day. His salesman said to him, "Sir, are you sure you can afford these?" Robbie snapped back, "I'll take TWO pair."

One evening Rockoff and I drove together to a concert on Long Island. On the way back to New York, we were listening to Jessie on the radio. Rockoff mentioned a story in the news about a radio station that was being sued for unauthorized airplay of a record. As I recall, it was a pop hit single by a major artist that the station had acquired prior to its release. Rockoff commented about how stupid they were to incur the legal expenses. At that moment, Jessie played a track from a bootleg album, *The Dylan/ Cash Sessions*, which consisted of then unreleased material recorded by Bob Dylan and Johnny Cash in Nashville. I turned the volume down and hoped that Rockoff didn't notice. When we got back to the station, I removed that track and all similar material from the studio.

The Bottom Line was a venue in Greenwich Village that sometimes presented country artists. Kris Kristofferson and his wife Rita Coolidge were one of the first acts I saw there. Billy Swan, who had the pop and country hit "I Can Help," was in their band at the time. Kristofferson had a No. 1 country hit, "Why Me," which crossed over to pop and became a million-seller, but he didn't have another hit until as a member of The Highwaymen with Waylon Jennings, Willie Nelson and Johnny Cash. A couple years later WHN would play Coolidge's "I'd Rather

Leave While I'm In Love." Although it was probably not aimed at the country market, it broke into the top forty on both the pop and country charts and was played on the album rock stations. Kristofferson became a movie star after starring with Barbra Streisand in *A Star Is Born* in a role reputedly turned down by Elvis Presley.

Eddy Arnold had a big WHN hit that year with "Cowboy." Arnold's hits had started in 1945 and he was elected to the Country Music Hall of Fame in 1968. Like Jim Reeves and Ray Price, he was one of the first artists who brought country music to a wider and more urban audience. He was in his late fifties at the time, and is one example of how WHN included older artists along with more contemporary performers on its deep playlist.

Larry Kenney's humor and gift for accurate impressions of newsmakers, brought a lot of listeners to WHN who wouldn't have come for country music alone. Larry also provided the voices of "Count Chocula" and "Sonny, the Coco-Puffs Coo-Coo Bird." Larry and WNBC morning personality Don Imus, for whom Larry had done voice impressions, recorded a comedy single, "Presidential Debate," released by Epic records as by Road Hog and Neon Cactus. Done in the style of Buchanan and Goodman's 1956 hit, "The Flying Saucer," the record consisted of questions from impersonated politicians, including Nixon, answered with cut-in snippets of recent Top 40 hits. Because most of the records used were not compatible with WHN, we didn't play it as much as we would have liked to as a way to promote Larry's morning show.

WHN was especially interested in giving airplay to local artists whose records fit the station. It was another way of connecting New York with country music. We got an opportunity when Paul Evans, who had had pop hits in the 60s with "Seven Little Girls Sitting In The Back Seat," "Happy Go Lucky Me," and "Midnight Special"(the latter two in oldies rotation at WHN), released a novelty song to celebrate America's bicentennial.

Ed Salamon

"Happy Birthday America" by Paul Evans reached the No. 1 position on WHN's charts that summer.

Based on the results of the April/May rating, WHN's transformation rated a feature story in the Business and Finance section of the July 4th issue of the *New York Times* titled, "Nashville's Bite of the Big Apple." The article began, "Can Country music make it in New York? That was the question for the Storer Broadcasting Company in 1973 . . . the answer two years later was a resounding 'no.'" The article reported that by 1975, the station was nearly a million dollars in the red, and had lost $700,000 on revenues that year and was "mired in 14th place . . . for the 25-49 year-old market." It continued: "Suddenly, however, the New York station is flying . . . it expects a profit of more than $500,000 this year. . . . It has skyrocketed in listenership to the No. 2 position among competitors and its 1.5 million listeners are eagerly sought by advertisers."

J. J. Ramey has been cited as the first black disc jockey at a major market country radio station. He recalls, "In the summer of 1976, I arrived in New York City with great ambition of continuing my career in radio. At first I had to settle for temporary, low-paying unsatisfying jobs. After sending out dozens of resumes and air checks, I had the feeling nothing would work. One day I took a chance and dropped off a resume and air check to 1050 WHN Radio Station located at 400 Park Avenue. A few hours before I was to show up at Macy's to be a gift wrapper (I had never wrapped a package that looked decent in my life!), I called my answering service and had a call from WHN program director Ed Salamon. He wanted to see me about a job. Wow. Maybe he would like me. Maybe this was the break I was looking for."

"The question I asked myself: would he really hire a black man to deejay on a big-city country station. And then it hit me: my first disc jockey job was a WDXN-AM Country in Clarksville, Tennessee. I had also anchored radio news on WKDA-AM

WHN: WHEN NEW YORK CITY WENT COUNTRY

Country in Nashville. When I arrived at Ed's office, he was super-friendly and very excited that I had not only worked at WKDA-AM & FM in Music City, but that I had actually worked in Nashville. Ed, who had so much energy and excitement all of the time, hired me for an overnight weekend deejay job, but to give me gainful employment, he put me on full-time nights doing what he called 'demographic research'—what a super title. I soon learned that I was a telephone answerer, but I didn't care, as long as I had a shot at WHN."

WHN initiated a Listeners Choice poll in which the audience would vote for their favorite artists in several categories. One category would be featured each week. These awards were prized by artists, especially Elvis Presley. The first time he won, Elvis sent a hand signed note of thanks to WHN general manager Neil Rockoff. To this day, two WHN Listeners Choice awards hang in the Hall of Gold in the Trophy Room at Graceland, where Elvis had them placed along with his earliest gold records and other most precious memorabilia. The awards are signed by me and Neil Rockoff; if I would have known where they would be displayed, I would have written a little clearer. One of the awards is visible in a photo on page 63 of the *Elvis Presley's Graceland; The Official Guidebook (Third Edition)*.

Alan Furst from Bethany College in West Virginia was a WHN intern this year. He had previously interned with me at WEEP in Pittsburgh and then with Charlie Cook when Charlie was programming WWVA. He went on to a very successful career as a multi-format program director and consultant, despite the fact that he once knocked over Pam Green's coffee in the music library, spilling it over some important papers and her.

In August, the *Village Voice* ran a cover story on Jessie. Her photo was captioned "She's New York's number two deejay" and noted "Jessie is short, sexily chunky, and could have been designed by R. Crumb. 'At broadcasting school, they said I had a chocolate throat.'"

About this time Jessie attracted the attention of a stalker. This was particularly disturbing because it came at the time of the attacks later known as the Son of Sam killings where young women in New York were being murdered by someone unknown to them. The stalker would send Jessie mail offering to meet her when she got off the air at midnight. WHN was concerned enough for her safety to provide her with an escort out of the building and a waiting cab to take her home. Eventually the calls and letters stopped and Jessie felt safe again.

Making an impact in a market is one thing, sustaining it is another. The cover of the August 30th issue of *Television Radio Age* proclaimed "Book after book, WHN has consistently been among the top three most popular radio stations in America's No. 1 market among adults 25-49 all week long."

Doug Sahm was a guest deejay on August 30th during Jessie's show. Doug, formerly leader of the Sir Douglas Quintet ("She's About A Mover" and "Mendocino") was recording country material for ABC/Dot records. Doug spent a lot of time in New York and his Quintet band mate Augie Meyers, who played the organ riffs on those songs, moved there too. Doug was an early riser and would invite me to "breakfast at Tiffany's," Tiffany's being a modest coffee shop in midtown Manhattan. Bob Dylan was a fan of Sahm's and I recall seeing him in the audience when Doug played at the Bottom Line. Sahm and I would pal around when he was in town, sometimes going to see live music together. I remember being with him at the Lone Star Café while the headlining act played Doug's signature song "She's About A Mover." I think they thought they were doing a tribute to Doug, but from the look on his face I don't think he appreciated their rendition.

Waylon Jennings was a frequent guest deejay on WHN until the album, *Wanted! The Outlaws*, became the first country album to sell a million copies. RCA decided to promote him as rock and would only let him appear on rock station WNEW-FM when he visited New York. As you might imagine, that was really frustrating to everyone at WHN, but the station continued to play his records because the listeners requested them. Eventually, RCA gave up trying to make him a rock star and Jennings returned to the WHN studios.

In October, *Billboard* ran the article "New York Embraces Country's New Breed" in it's "The World Of Country Music" section. *Billboard* said, "Quite possibly the most important motivating factor in the birth of New York country music was, and still is, WHN country radio. In the past year, under the guidance of Neil Rockoff, this 50,000 watter has been converting all kinds of people to country music. In fact, country music in New York can no longer be pushed aside as only belonging to Southerners and 'hillbillies,' since it is now 'everyone's music.'"

Barry Kluger joined the creative services department that year. Kluger recalls, "My first professional job ever was at WHN where I was hired by Dale Pon, the legendary radio promotion and marketing executive. I started on September 13th, a Monday, and showed up for my job as a promotion assistant, having worked in college radio and local public relations firms in Washington. A few months earlier, I had a college friend who was a desk clerk at a local hotel stuff my resume into the room mailboxes of radio executives attending a convention. Only one person got back to me a few weeks later and that was Dale. I came to New York that summer and interviewed with Dale who was both engaging and frightening. Needless to say, he saw something in me that kick started a successful thirty-five year career in communications. What stood out, though, was that first day when I went out for my first three hour lunch with the folks from Ringling Bros., with whom WHN was doing a promotion. It was my first martini which started a trend that exists to this day and made three-hour lunches a benchmark of my 'illustrious legacy.'"As part of the WHN promotion that Kluger and Pon arranged that day, Bob Wayne, Del De Montreux and Pam Green rode elephants in the Ringling Bros. and Barnum & Bailey Circus parade to Nassau Coliseum. Pictures appeared in the local newspaper.

Lee Arnold was named the Country Music Association Major Market Disc Jockey of the Year. A press report said that this was the first time an air personality from a northern market had won that honor. Country radio was no longer the regional format that it once was considered.

The December 5th issue of the *Sunday News* carried a feature headlined "Jessie, a sweet talkin' woman." Writer Jean Perry noted that Jessie was the only woman disc jockey on AM radio in the market. She revealed that friends started calling her Jessie because of her habit of wearing dungarees, a fringed jacket, a cowboy hat and spurred boots; Jessie sounded Western.

Another WHN hit that would probably not be played on radio in today's more politically correct times was "C.B. Savage" by Rod Hart, a novelty song which featured CB radio operator sounding stereotypically gay ("Yoo hoo, breakeroo"). It made it into the top thirty on country charts and nearly halfway up the pop charts. Plantation Records issued the single on a pink, rather than their usual green, label.

WHN's No. 1 song of the year was "Teddy Bear" by Red Sovine. Rounding out the top five were "Sometimes" by Bill Anderson and Mary Lou Turner, "The Winner" by Bobby Bare, "Without Your Love (Mr. Jordan)" by Charlie Ross, and "Paloma Blanca" by the George Baker Selection.

Before it became a country station, WHN was perhaps best known for *The Original Amateur Hour*, the predecessor of talent shows such as *The Gong Show*, *American Idol* and *The Voice*. The show was the creation of WHN manager Major Edward Bowes and was carried by the CBS radio network from 1936 until the end of its run on radio in 1952.

WHN deejays Bruce Bradley, Del De Montreux, Stan Martin and Dan Daniel surround Johnny Cash (fourth from left) at his 1973 concert at the C. W. Post campus of Long Island University in Nassau County.(Courtesy Frank D'Elia)

Bill Anderson performed at WHN's 1973 Family Picnic at the Queens campus of St. John's University. Pictured left to right are deejays Del De Montreux, Lee Arnold, Stan Martin, Jack Spector, Bruce Bradley, Steve Warren, Dan Daniel and Anderson. (Courtesy Frank D'Elia)

WHN program director, and later station manager, Ruth Meyer (seated) shown with Jack Spector and Barbara Mandrell in 1973. (Courtesy Frank D'Elia)

Johnny Cash was a frequent visitor to and good friend of WHN. He was in New York so often during the 70s, that he had an apartment on Central Park South. Ed Salamon is pictured with Cash in the WHN studios shortly after Ed's arrival.

Del De Montreux and Jessie welcome C. W. McCall to his first appearance as a WHN guest deejay. His 1975 hit "Convoy" reached No. 1 on both the country and pop charts and later inspired the motion picture starring Kris Kristofferson and Ali MacGraw.

Charlie Daniels shares a laugh with Jessie and Epic Records promotion man Ray Free in front of a WHN subway poster featuring Freddy Fender. The poster, in Spanish, was used in high density Hispanic neighborhood subway stations. Because of this and other outreaches to Hispanic listeners, WHN had a large Latino audience.

Mel Tillis (right) sits in as a guest deejay with Del De Montreux, who is wearing a t-shirt promoting Mel's latest album on MGM Records "M-M-Mel." Tillis was known for his stutter, which always made for an interesting time when he was guest deejay.

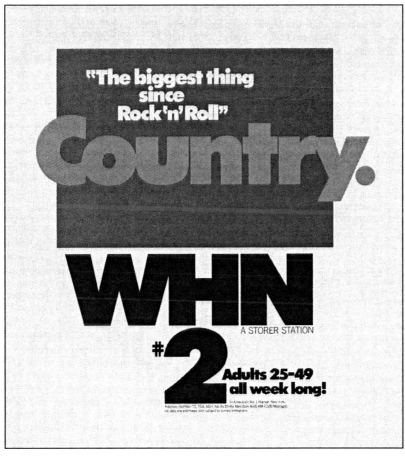

WHN ran this advertisement in industry trade publications after the station's turnaround in the fall 1975 ratings. It heralded WHN's success with the age group most sought after by advertisers. The reference to Rock 'n' Roll positioned the station directly behind WABC, the Top 40 station which at that time was the most listened to station in the USA.

As interest in western wear grew in the mid 70s, WHN produced heavy brass belt buckles with its logo. The buckles became one of the most popular contest prizes ever awarded by the station.

Marty Robbins sat in as guest deejay in 1976. He is surrounded by Ed Salamon (left), Neil Rockoff and Bob Wayne.

Waylon Jennings was a frequent guest deejay on WHN until the album *Wanted! The Outlaws* became the first country album to sell a million copies. RCA decided to promote him as rock and would only let him appear on WNEW-FM. Like Tom T. Hall, Bill Anderson, Willie Nelson and others, Waylon had worked as a deejay, so he seems comfortable behind the WHN mike circa 1976.

CHAPTER FIVE
1977

"The King is Gone" – Ronnie McDowell (1977)

I was named to the newly created position of national program director of Storer Radio this year. In addition to WHN, Storer's stations included KTNQ (10-Q) and KGBS-FM, Los Angeles; WLAK-FM, Chicago; WGBS and WLYF-FM, Miami and WTOD, Toledo. Since KGBS-FM was also a country station, I was now programming country stations in America's top two markets. Storer wanted me to focus on their Los Angeles stations and they rented a home for me in Granada Hills, near LA, so that I could temporarily relocate there. I kept my title as WHN program director and WHN's assistant program director filled in for me during my absences.

Don Imus was partner in a restaurant/bar, Imus, on 54th Street around the corner from the radio station. The WHN staff decided to have a party there to celebrate my promotion. I was busy at work, so they started without me. When I went to join them, I was stopped at the door. Imus had a dress code and I was wearing jeans, which was not permitted. In this pre-cell phone era, I had to ask someone to go in and tell them that I could not attend my own party.

At this time, Neil Rockoff was promoted to the newly created position of president of the radio division and Dale Pon to national creative services director. Neil Rockoff promoted Nick Verbitsky to WHN general manger and Nick promoted Brian Moors from the sales department to general sales manger. Pon hired Frcd Siebert to run the creative services department while he was out of town.

Pam Green recalls, "I believe Larry Gatlin made his first guest deejay appearance at WHN on January 4th. He is one of the artists that I have had a long friendship with. I first met him at Narwood Productions where Lee Arnold was recording his syndicated radio show *Country Cookin.*' Actually, it was in the building elevator. I told Lee that I wanted to meet Larry, so he let me tag along with him." Larry was probably a guest deejay at WHN more than any other artist.

D. J. MacLaughlan of the Agency for the Performing Arts was a WHN listener who became a good friend of the station. He told me that he signed his first country act, Larry Gatlin, after hearing one of his records on WHN while exiting the Lincoln Tunnel when commuting from New Jersey to Manhattan. Gatlin was the first of many country artists that would be signed by APA.

Sid Bernstein, who presented the Beatles' first American concert at Carnegie Hall in 1964, was another WHN listener. I met him when he began booking acts at Radio City Music Hall. They included a number of country artists, opening another New York venue for the music. Many country artists consider their performances at Radio City Music Hall, as well as Carnegie Hall, as the highlight of their career. I am confident that most of those booking wouldn't have happened without their exposure on WHN.

WHN's new advertising campaign slogan was "Thank you for being a part of our country." The inference was that the artist pictured was thanking the listener. This campaign featured the usual stars, plus the Eagles, who were certainly not core artists for any other country radio station.

On May 13th, Dolly Parton began a three night stand at the Bottom Line. Jessie remembers, "There had been the noisy declaration of her parting with Porter Wagoner, which was to set the stage for her solo career, and further there was a move to create a scenario that would carry Dolly into the mainstream. There was a huge hit with "Here You Come Again," and a *Playboy* magazine cover. Dolly was making the rounds, including trips to the major media markets to grow her exposure. We at WHN Radio in New York City had played host to her. She graced us on the air as a guest deejay, and later, I was part of the radio station staff that accompanied her to Atlantic City for a video shoot as promotion for the radio station. I was in attendance when Dolly played The Bottom Line in 1977, and after that amazing show there was a glittering after-party at the top of The World Trade Towers.

"My most favorite Dolly memory happened one night, when she declared that she wanted to go to Studio 54. I acted as the guide for the entourage. Back in those days, the doormen/bouncers kept careful watch on the rowdy masses looking to penetrate the barricades to gain entrance into this gilded palace of sin. It was all that! Beautiful women, VIPs, and power brokers of all stripes, in essence the Who's Who of New York, were let in almost as Noah curated the animals for the Ark. If you went with the glitterati, you would be granted admission, other nights, they would likely ignore you, up against the velvet ropes calling out like baby birds waiting for their parents to feed them. The night I went with Dolly, the ropes parted and the doors opened wide. We trooped inside and made our way up to the seats in the balcony. Studio 54 was housed in an old theater, and the seats on the first floor had all been removed to make way for dancing. Pulsating light poles descended from the ceiling. That wasn't all that was descending at the legendary nightclub. Sex, drugs, and rock and roll, well actually it was DISCO, baby; all this debauchery, in flagrant delicto, right before your eyes. Seriously, people were not just doing things behind closed bathroom stalls. Much of the depravity could quite easily be watched. And make no mistake, we were witnessing, whether we wanted to or not. I don't think we made it past the half hour mark, when Dolly turned to me and pronounced in her unforgettable voice, 'This place is like Sodom and Gomorrah! We gotta get out of here before the Lord strikes us all down.' And so the entourage all stood and we filed out and dispersed into the night."

I also attended Dolly's after party at the Windows On The World restaurant following her debut performance at the Bottom Line. At one point I found myself standing near Mick Jagger. I had briefly met Jagger in 1964 when the Rolling Stones had played Westview Park Danceland in Pittsburgh. They had not yet had their first hit and the crowd was small, so even as a sixteen year old I was able to make my way to the backstage area and chat with the Stones before their show. When I approached Mick this evening, his eyes seemed to be glazed over and his speech incomprehensible to me. I quickly gave up on having a conversation.

On Wednesday, May 25th, WHN air personalities participated in a "WHN Night At The Meadowlands" promotion at that New Jersey racetrack. Del De Montreux, Ed Baer, Lee Arnold and Bob Wayne participated in a harness race against each other driving sulky carts pulled by horses. De Montreux won and was presented with a trophy.

WHN broadcast a live show with Tammy Wynette from Central Park in July. It was a free show and the park was packed with WHN listeners and probably a lot of concert goers that were new to the station. Wynette was not only one of country music's biggest artist, but her recent divorce from George Jones had caused tabloid coverage that had made her name a household word.

Charlie Cook replaced Robbie Roman as assistant program director. Robbie wanted to return to Pittsburgh and I was able to arrange for Robbie to be program director at country formatted WIXZ as part of a consulting deal I had with that station. Robbie was quoted in the *Pittsburgh Press* saying, "I just want to do country the way its being done at WHN and the way it was done at WEEP under Salamon."

I first met Cook the previous year at an industry convention in New Orleans and was impressed by him. He tells the story that he asked, "Can I hang around with you, maybe I'll learn something." Charlie was already program director at legendary country station WWVA in Wheeling, home of the Wheeling Jamboree, so he was already quite accomplished.

While I was in Los Angeles, Larry Gatlin was again a guest deejay at WHN. I received a call saying that after a contest promo Gatlin had said something like, "I don't know why you bother to enter, nobody wins these things anyway." That made me mad enough to call Gatlin's manager to complain. That made Gatlin mad and he asked why I didn't complain to him directly. I had no way of doing that, but I did know his manager D. J. MacLaughlin. The disagreement resulted in reciprocal threats of physical violence. Coincidentally, Gatlin was scheduled to stop by the 10-Q/KGBS studios shortly afterwards. When I saw him in my doorway, I ordered the door closed. As I recall, there was some shouting and perhaps even some shoving, but we have been friends ever since.

WHN was able to negotiate a contract with AFTRA and IBEW permitting air talent to run their own equipment. The studio was rebuilt, which took from February through June. At that point, all the air talent went combo, except for Larry Kenney.

Having an engineer to run the board had not always been an advantage for the deejays. J. J. Ramey remembers his first air shift: "This would be the first time I had ever worked with an engineer running the controls and now I knew I was in the big time. The engineer was a 'jolly' Black man with a gap in between his two front teeth and he was constantly joking, laughing and happy. He assured me that I would be alright on-air and that he would help me through the transitions. I soon learned what he meant. I gave the signal to the engineer to open my microphone. The on-air light came on, and he immediately grabbed a *Playboy* magazine, held it high in front of me and the centerfold featuring a naked model tumbled open as I began to speak. My mouth dropped open and I was shocked that he would do such a thing. I never stumbled over a single word but I knew my eyes were as big as baseballs or bigger. The jolly engineer almost fell out of his chair laughing at me. I kept talking and after my first break ended, we both laughed it off. He must have had every *Playboy*, every *Penthouse*, and every other magazine that featured naked 'ladies' ever published. All night he revealed centerfold after centerfold to me and by the time I got home and went to sleep, I counted naked *Playboy* bunnies instead of counting sheep!"

Peter Kanze recalls that shortly after the new studio was completed, Bob Wayne threw up on the brand new McCurdy console. According to Kanze, Wayne had eaten some bad seafood for lunch. After a few seconds of dead air, staffers went to the studio to see what the matter was. Fortunately, Lee Arnold was still at the station and took over from the interview studio, which was under construction.

With me spending so much time in LA, I felt it only fair to Charlie Cook that I fire Bob "the Wizard" Wayne. Wayne would sometimes smell of alcohol and appear to be drunk when he came into the station. I had had to send him home as being in no condition to go on the air. I thought so highly of him as an air talent, that I was willing to do a daily "Wizard check" with him before he went on the air. I thought that was too much to ask from Cook. After leaving WHN, Bob Wayne joined adult contemporary WYNY.

Mike Fitzgerald, who was doing overnights at WCBS-FM, replaced Wayne. We knew from analysis of the ratings that the station that WHN shared the most listeners with was WCBS-FM. That was surprising because normally stations would share listeners with other stations on the same band of the dial (AM stations with other AM stations). However, WHN did play a lot of crossover oldies and, at the time, many listeners might have had FM radios at home, but not in their cars. Mike Fitzgerald was a familiar voice to a large portion of the WHN audience.

It was common for WHN air personalities to socialize with country artists. Larry Gatlin recalls that he once rode with Larry Kenney to a George Jones and Tammy Wynette show in Long Island. As it got later, Kenney left to get some sleep before his morning show. Gatlin was to get a ride back to Manhattan on George Jones' tour bus. That bus left Gatlin off at Lenox Avenue in Harlem at 3:00 am from which Gatlin tried to flag down a cab, scarce in that neighborhood at that time of night. When a cab finally did appear, Gatlin remembers the driver asking him "What are you doing HERE, white boy?"

Sportscaster Bill Mazer's contract was up and we looked for someone who could present sports in a more contemporary manner. Bill was known as the "A-Maz-In" Mazer for his encyclopedia knowledge of sports trivia. Pete Kanze suggested that I listen to Sports Phone, a dial-a-score service which was being voiced by Howie Rose, a recent graduate of Queens College. Rose had the contemporary sound we wanted and he replaced Mazur.

Howie Rose remembers: "I actually had a special fondness for WHN dating back to 1967, ten years before I was hired. That summer, my friends and I started a fan club for Marv Albert, who was working at the station doing Rangers and Knicks games. Occasionally, Marv invited us (really, we invited ourselves) to come to the station for a tour, and just to see how things worked. I was thirteen-years-old, a typical adolescent, and the station's switchboard operator was an extremely attractive, well-proportioned redhead named Carol. She was gorgeous. Our visits to

WHN were always a treat, not only to see Marv, but to gawk at Carol. Ten years later, when I was brought in for my job interview, I wondered if she would be at the switchboard, but by then she no longer worked there. Several years later, perhaps fifteen years after I had first seen her, a similarly attractive but obviously older redhead was being shown the nuances of WHN's new, modernized switchboard. Incredibly, it was her. She was returning to her old job. I introduced myself and she got a kick out of the story. That night, I saw Marv at the Knicks game, and when I told him that Carol was back at the station he replied, 'That's the comeback story of the year.'

"My first appearance on WHN as the morning sportscaster was on the morning drive show on Memorial Day, 1977. Larry Kenney was the morning drive deejay and Gene Ladd was the newscaster. I hadn't gotten to know Larry very well at that point. When he brought me on for my very first sports report, he introduced me as Howie 'Ross.' In that split second one has to decide how to handle such things, my choices were either to let it go or correct him and hope he wouldn't be embarrassed and become angry. I chose the latter and simply said, 'Actually, that's Rose.' Larry was extremely apologetic; couldn't have been nicer, but I had to be a wise guy anyway and replied to his apology, 'That's okay, Ron.' Thankfully, he laughed, and seemed to get a kick out of the exchange. When I walked out of the news booth, after a moment I had waited my whole life for, Gene was waiting for me with a little grin, and in that John Wayne cowboy drawl of his said, 'You're good, kid.' I will never forget how great those three words made me feel. Gene was one of the people I had met years before when I visited the station to see Marv Albert, so to have his immediate approval was a remarkable feeling."

The Association of Country Entertainers (ACE) requested that the Country Music Association examine the classification of WHN as a full-time country music station. In 1977, WHN was sharing a lot of its music with the biggest radio station in

America, Top 40 WABC, which perennially ranked first among 25-49 adult listeners, the audience most desired by radio advertisers. WHN's music research tested songs that were doing well with our competitors and WHN listeners told us which of those songs they thought fit WHN. As a result, that year WHN played songs that were intended for pop radio including "Margaritaville" by Jimmy Buffett, "After The Lovin" by Englebert Humperdinck, "New Kid In Town" by the Eagles and "The Wreck of The Edmund Fitzgerald" by Gordon Lightfoot. These records not only took up places on the WHN charts that ACE members felt Nashville based music was entitled to, but all of those records also took up places on the national country charts as country stations who followed what WHN played added the records as well. ACE had been formed in 1974 after a meeting at George Jones and Tammy Wynette's house after the CMA awards. The concern was that awards were being won by artists who were not traditional country and were not based in Nashville. The gathering included Dolly Parton, Barbara Mandrell, Bill Anderson and Conway Twitty, who ironically themselves had crossed over onto the pop charts. The CMA never addressed ACE's concern about WHN.

Perhaps it was because the CMA was aware of the even greater benefit WHN was having in spreading Nashville based music to pop radio. WABC's music list was based on the best selling single records in the New York area. Before call-out research existed, stations would call record shops and ask them for a list of their best selling records. As WHN's audience grew, the station began to have a considerable impact on single record sales in the New York area. When WABC detected these sales in their store research, they were encouraged to add the records. As America's biggest radio station, other Top 40 station followed what WABC played, so a song added to WABC was added at virtually every Top 40 radio station. Country records played by WABC that year included "Here You Come Again" by Dolly Parton, "Lucille" by

Ed Salamon

Kenny Rogers, "You Light Up My Life" by Debby Boone and "Don't It Make My Brown Eyes Blue" by Crystal Gayle. All became sizable pop hits. WABC program director Rick Sklar and I had become friends. We often spoke at the same events and attended the same industry gatherings. Sklar had worked at WHN before he programmed WABC. I appreciated the many opportunities I had to talk with him about programming and to learn his theories behind what he'd done at WABC.

Randy Barlow was a former pop singer who had worked on Dick Clark's Caravan of Stars. His backers, Fred and Barbara Kelly, had him record older pop songs in a country style and his versions of Gene Pitney's hit, "Twenty Four Hours From Tulsa," and Neil Diamond's "Kentucky Woman" worked great on WHN. He later recorded original material which was even more successful for him, giving him a string of top ten national country hits.

"Let Your Love Flow" by the Bellamy Brothers also did better on WHN than other country stations. It initially charted on the pop charts, where it eventually reached No. 1. Although it peaked at about twenty on the national country charts, it became a frequently played oldie after their later successes. Whenever I see David and Howard they often bring up the first time we met. Even though they are about my age, they were nervous about meeting me so they needed to relax and when I entered their hotel room it was like going onto Willie Nelson's bus. One of their later hits "Get Into Reggae Cowboy" was inspired during a trip to New York when a man in dreadlocks shouted out that phrase to them while they were walking in midtown Manhattan.

Another single that WHN listeners liked more than the national country audience was a version of "You Are My Sunshine" credited to Duane Eddy and Friends. The friends included Willie Nelson, Waylon Jennings and wife Jessi Colter (Duane's ex-wife), Kin Vassey (from the First Edition), and Duane's current wife, Deed Abbate. Duane's instrumental "Rebel Rouser" had been a country hit, and was played as an oldie on WHN, but Waylon and Willie had the golden touch with WHN listeners, and so WHN played almost everything they recorded.

The April 16th issue of *Billboard* ran an article headlined "Salamon's Success" which reported on a lecture I gave at the New School for Social Research and quoted me as crediting WHN's success to playing music targeted to a specific adult audience, compared with Top 40 stations, which had a broader target audience.

"Country Comes To Carnegie Hall" was a live concert with Roy Clark, Don Williams, Freddy Fender and Hank Thompson that was recorded for an ABC/Dot record album and originated as a syndicated live concert broadcast by WHN. About thirty stations, including WMAQ, Chicago, carried the broadcast on May 17th, which was distributed live over telephone lines. The album was released near the end of the year. The acts were managed by Jim Halsey, who would later guide the Oak Ridge Boys' career. ABC/Dot vice president promotion, Larry Baunach, did most of the work lining up both artists and stations.

Jimmy Buffett's "Margaritaville" became a big WHN record and hit single on both country and pop charts, However, Buffett seemed to me to be more of a pop act. I didn't see him at country events. In fact, to this day I have never met him.

We kept a close ear on other New York stations for any country music they might be exposing. For example, the progressive rock station, WNEW-FM, played many of the country rock records that Jessie played on WHN in the evenings. We noticed that Don Imus had been playing "Nobody Wants To Play Rhythm Guitar Behind Jesus" by the Oak Ridge Boys, a gospel quartet that been touring with Johnny Cash. Imus' morning show on WNBC was successful and since both his station and WHN were on the AM dial, we shared a lot of listeners. WHN began playing the record. Then in the summer of 1977, the Oak Ridge Boys switched labels to ABC/Dot and took a serious run at being a mainstream country act. Their first single was "Y'all Come Back Saloon." Since the act was already well known to the WHN audience, we began playing the record immediately. It became a huge nationwide country hit. The Oak Ridge Boys still to this day remember and greet me whenever they see me at industry functions. In 1981, WHN would also help break their platinum selling single "Elvira." By that time, their new records were automatic additions to country radio playlists, but the single sales in New York from WHN airplay helped to cross that song over to Top 40 radio.

Over the years, "You Light Up My Life" by Debby Boone has become one of the records people love to hate. That is probably due to the huge amount of airplay it received when it was released. Debby Boone is the daughter of Pat Boone and the granddaughter of Country Music Hall of Famer Red Foley. The record was promoted by Ray Ruff, a former singer who was mentored by Buddy Holly and originally produced by Holly's producer Norman Petty. Ruff once had a record delivered to WHN in a Brinks security truck as a promotional stunt to underscore the importance on giving WHN an exclusive on it. WHN music director Pam Green and the air personalities were present at our weekly music meeting and agreed unanimously that "You Light Up My Life" was a hit and it went right on the air. Later that year, Debby received the Grammy for Best New Artist and I received a gold record award for breaking the record, which went on to become a platinum seller.

I don't believe there was payola in country radio. If it existed, I think I would have been offered it at WHN, and I never was. Records move up the charts according to a combination of sales and airplay. The value of the airplay is weighted by the importance of the station. There was no country station with a greater weighting than WHN. Record label representatives would often take me and music director Pam Green to lunch or dinner, so that they would have the opportunity to tell us about their records and artists. We would be given tickets to see artists when they played in the New York area. However, I was never made to feel that I was obligated beyond listening to their pitch or music. There was never a quid pro quo for airplay. Music was added by Pam and me at a weekly music meeting, based on what we thought our listeners would want to hear, sometimes with input from interested WHN air personalities. Lee Arnold and Jessie, especially, would listen to and see a lot of music and so could call things to our attention. It then moved up our chart based on local sales, requests and the results of our call out research. Our value as professionals was in our ability to attract and keep an audience. It would be very short term thinking to take something to play a record that wasn't the best choice. The real money was in a program director's continued paycheck and career. That said, I was never tempted as I was never offered anything of value to play a record on WHN.

Likewise, I also never received any offers to work at record companies. When I worked for a Congressman in Pittsburgh, I became aware that lobbyists would often offer jobs with their firms to Congressional staff members "once they were finished working on The Hill." It was a subtle way of gaining their co-operation. Likewise, I noticed cooperative radio program and music directors being hired by record companies, but, not being ones to follow the label's game plans, neither Pam Green nor I were ever even approached.

Even though it was a big station in America's No. 1 market, WHN was not immune to the mistakes that happened at stations everywhere. Bernie Wagenblast remembers running taped programs on Sunday morning from two reel-to-reel tape decks in the main studio. "The first program ended and as I switched to the next I quickly discovered the tape and been reversed and was tails out, meaning the show was airing backwards! All listeners are hearing is a bunch of gibberish. I spun around and grabbed a song from the cart rack and quickly put it on the air. Listeners who were expecting to hear *The Lutheran Hour* were probably shocked to hear Dolly Parton on their radios. I rewound the tape as quickly as possible, reversed the tape and brought it back on the air. I potted Dolly down and brought up the tape and then heard, 'Stations, our program begins in 30 seconds.' Once again I potted down the show and brought the music back up while I advanced the tape to the actual start of the show. Being that I was the new kid on the block I figured I had reached the end of my short-lived career. Fortunately, my boss Charlie Kaye, was forgiving and I lived to see another day."

In June, Lee Arnold launched *Country Corner*, a new one hour weekly artist interview show for Narwood Productions, the same company that syndicated his weekly two hour *Country Cookin'* show.

Richie Allen Seinfeld, no relation to Jerry, was a postal worker and country music fan who I met through Pete Kanze. Seinfeld would save his money and each year promote a concert with a legendary country artist through his "Friends of Country" non-profit organization. These concerts were usually free to the public. On June 28th, Kitty Wells appeared on WHN as a guest deejay before performing at one of these concerts in Central Park with Lee Arnold as master of ceremonies.

The cover of the July 4th issue of *Broadcasting* magazine was an ad celebrating WHN as "The Second Biggest Radio Station In All The World: Adults 25-49," based on average quarter hour audience in the latest ratings. We were again second to WABC, and we were the biggest country radio station ever. Joe Bonsall of the Oak Ridge Boys was from nearby Philadelphia and appreciated what an achievement that was: "Now, with due respect, Boston had a station but it was not very successful and my home town city had a great country station as well but unfortunately it was 50 watts of power right down into the subway and quite frankly from Baltimore to Bangor country radio struggled with ratings with the exception of WHN! What KZLA was becoming to Los Angeles and WWWW to Detroit it seemed that WHN was doing that and even more right in the core of the Big Apple itself."

On July 13th at about 9:30 pm, the city experienced a black-out. I was on my way home, but it took a while to get out of the city with no stoplights or street lighting. I went right home and picked up a bunch of country records that I had there. I called Lee Arnold and asked him to meet me at the transmitter site. I had remembered that there was a small emergency studio at WHN's Secaucus, New Jersey transmitter that had a turntable, so we could broadcast from there. We went back on the air within hours and tried to simulate the WHN music mix as closely as possible. Mass transportation was disrupted and many people couldn't make it to work the following day. It was not until late in the evening of the 14th that all the power was restored. Pete Kanze taped the station from home. Since the logging tapes at the station did not have power and there were no station logs at the transmitter, Pete's tapes were the only record of what was broadcast that day. Neil Rockoff and chief engineer Bob Walton made sure that Pete had a case of blank tapes in case a similar emergency ever happened.

GRT records, which had country artists including Bobby G. Rice, Earl Thomas Conley and Alabama on their roster, released a double entendre novelty song "Telephone Man" by Meri Wilson. When we played it, listeners called wanting to hear it again and again. It became a No. 1 record at WHN that summer and a top fifty country hit nationally. It was a top ten pop hit and I received a gold record for breaking it when it had sold more than a million copies.

One of the biggest country hits of the year was a song written by Don Imus' brother Fred; "I Don't Want To Have To Marry You" by Jim Ed Brown and Helen Cornelius. Jim Ed was the lead singer of the Browns, who had the crossover hits "The Three Bells" and "Scarlet Ribbons" and "The Old Lamplighter" beginning in the late 50s before Jim established himself as a solo artist. This led to a string of hits for the duo, which still sometime perform together today.

Charlie Cook and I attended the *Billboard* International Programming Forum in Toronto in August. Larry Kenney was named Major Market Country Personality, I was named Major Market Country Program Director and Charlie Cook was named Medium Market Country Personality for his work at WWVA.

Howie Rose remembers: "Larry Kenney was a riot. In the middle of talking into or out of a record, he would kill his own microphone and say something off colored and switch the mike back on without breaking stride. Those of us in the studio had a great laugh, and Larry never slipped up. In retrospect, that's remarkable. The summer of 1977 in New York was fraught with fear because of the serial killer Son of Sam. Just a day or two before he was finally caught, a police sketch was released and was printed as a full page front page on New York's tabloid newspapers. I generally arrived for work in the 5:30 a.m. vicinity and was rarely even close to being awake. When I showed up this morning, the first person I saw in this mostly dark area of the station was a man walking around with the police sketch made into a mask. I almost hit the ceiling. Naturally, it was Larry. Another morning, Larry and engineer Joe Ellis combined to frighten a couple of newscasters named Susan Dempsey and Linda Lewis out of their skin. There was a terrorist group at the time known as the FALN. Susan and Linda were sweet, straight laced women and Larry and Joe knew this. The men conspired to call the newsroom, knowing that one of the women would answer the phone, and while disguising their voices said, 'This is the FALN and we are coming to the station. . . .' Before the sentence was even finished, Larry and Joe heard the screams through the supposedly soundproof door and quickly confessed before police could swarm the station."

In August, Don Imus left WNBC as part of the station wide

talent change. We had discussions about hiring him for mornings on WHN. His morning show had more listeners than ours and Don honestly loved country music. Ultimately we decided to stick with Larry Kenney, because of concerns about how Don's irreverent humor would be accepted by our audience. Instead, Imus spent about a year at WHK, a country station in Cleveland before returning to WNBC.

Elvis Presley died on August 16th. I had taken the afternoon off to see *Star Wars* with my son Eddie, who was visiting from Pittsburgh, and RCA record rep Dave Morrell. When the news came over the printer, WHN dispatched one of the station's engineers to get me out of the theater. He arrived just as the movie was getting out. We hurried back to the station and began wall to wall Elvis programming, collecting interviews with his friends and family. We sent copies of these interviews to other stations that requested them, including WEEP in Pittsburgh and WFEC, Harrisburg. Pam Green went to Memphis on the next available flight, and she provided a stream of interviews with fans. All the hotel rooms in Memphis were sold out and Pam wound up sleeping in the room of some sympathetic fans she met at the gates of Graceland. Eddie slept on the couch in my office that night as we continued to gather material. Our activities that day were memorialized in the book *When Elvis Died* by Neal and Janice Gregory, which documents the media coverage in the wake of his death. Elvis was scheduled to play his next concert at the Nassau Coliseum on Long Island on August 22nd, and I was supposed to meet him backstage.

There were many tribute records issued to honor Elvis. WHN played a number of them, including "Goodbye King Of Rock And Roll" by Leon Everette. Leon would later sign with RCA records and have more than a half dozen top ten country hits including "Giving Up Easy," "Hurricane" and "Midnight Rodeo." However, the biggest tribute was Ronnie McDowell's "The King Is Gone" on the tiny Scorpion label. This was another example of an independent artist and label that received immediate play on WHN. Our listener feedback through call out research enabled us to take chances and play records before they were proven elsewhere. Listeners would let us know whether or not we made a good choice. The record became both a pop and country hit and I received a gold record for it. Although McDowell would never have another pop hit, he had a long career in country radio with almost twenty top twenty hits, including "Wandering Eyes," "Older Women," and "You're Gonna Ruin My Bad Reputation." He lived in Portland, Tennessee, near Nashville, where he owned a restaurant that specialized in country cooking. McDowell loved to paint and cook as well as sing. He had decorated the restaurant with murals of the town and their world famous strawberry fields. Some years later, McDowell cooked dinner for me there. That meal was the first time I had ever eaten rabbit. It tasted like chicken to me.

WHN's 1977 ad campaign, created by Dale Pon, used the slogan "WHN gives you music you wanna hear" featured what was reported in the trade publications as the first authorized use of Elvis Presley's name and likeness to promote a radio station. An accompanying television spot utilized archive press conference film of Elvis. Other artists in this campaign included Kenny Rogers, Johnny Cash and Linda Ronstadt.

On September 23rd, Kris Kristofferson and Rita Coolidge performed at the Bottom Line. Pam Green and I attended and posed for photos with them backstage after the show. Kristofferson's "Why Me" had been a big country and pop hit in 1973, and was still played regularly on WHN. Although he was not able to follow that up with other country hits, he was also one of the many singer/songwriters whose album tracks were played on Jessie's show. Coolidge was just coming off a major WHN hit "We're All Alone," which did well on the pop, but not the country charts.

In October, I attended the annual Deejay Convention in Nashville. It was a celebration of the Grand Ole Opry's birthday and

WHN: When New York City Went Country

the opportunity for record labels to showcase their acts to country radio. One night Pam Green, Bob Pittman and I went to The Pickin' Parlor, a club at the corner of 2nd Avenue and Broadway. A new songwriter, Don Schlitz, was performing there. He sang his composition "The Gambler" and I knew it was a hit song. I thought it would be perfect for Gene Watson, who had recent success with story songs. I wrote "The Gambler," Gene Watson and Don Schwartz (which is how I thought I had heard Schlitz's name announced) on a Pickin' Parlor napkin. I meant to get in touch with Gene, but misplaced the napkin until years later. I wonder if it would have made a difference in his career, or in the career of Kenny Rogers, who had the hit with that song the following year.

That same month, I received a two page hand written letter from Randy Owen on Wildcountry, Inc. stationery asking me to listen to the new record "I Wanna Be With You Tonight" by his group, Alabama, on GRT records and giving me his home phone number and address in Myrtle Beach, where they were appearing at The Bowery, as well as in Fort Payne, Alabama, in case I wanted to be in touch. According to the letterhead, the group consisted of Randy, Jeff Cook, Teddy Gentry and Rick Scott. We listened, but didn't hear it as a hit. However, three years later I remembered Owen's letter and listened to Alabama's "My Home's In Alabama" on the independent MDJ record label and added it.

That fall, Paul Simon released the single "Slip Slidin' Away" on which he was backed by the Oak Ridge Boys as part of his *Greatest Hits, Etc.* album. WHN jumped on it even before the Top 40 stations, announcing it as by the Oak Ridge Boys with Paul Simon. It was a top five pop hit but never made the country charts.

Mel Tillis, the Oak Ridge Boys and Donna Fargo headlined a "New York Country" show on November 28th. It was once a rarity for country artists to play New York City, but by now it was a common occurrence. There was an after party at Giorgio's, an upscale restaurant in the area.

Don Williams appeared at the Bottom Line on December 7th. It was still a rush to see country acts, especially those who hadn't received airplay on other formats, being booked at this venue renown for presenting the biggest rock acts. Country music was hotter than it had ever been in New York City. After the show there was a party at nearby Pirandello's.

My friend and fellow Pittsburgher, Joe Rock, who managed The Skyliners ("Since I Don't Have You") introduced me to Gary Knight and Gene Allan. Gene had been a member of The Tempos ("See You In September") and had co-written Bobby Vinton's hit "Mr. Lonely." The duo had written a narration, "A Trucker's Christmas," capitalizing on the CB fad. I felt that it would be perfect for Lee Arnold and they produced it with him and released it on the Kirschner label, where they were working. WHN first played the original version, but switched to a custom version in which the "Merry Christmas to everyone" ending was changed to "Merry Christmas, WHN." It was written with as much CB slang as possible and some of the language, such as "on my way to the Sears and Roebuck to buy my beaver a gift," seems strange today. Although the record didn't become a hit, it was a great way to promote WHN's midday air personality throughout the day.

"Lucille" by Kenny Rogers topped WHN's Top 105 of 1977. It was followed by "Don't It Make My Brown Eyes Blue" by Crystal Gayle, "It Was Almost like a Song" by Ronnie Milsap, "Torn Between Two Lovers" by Mary MacGregor and "Luckenbach, Texas" by Waylon (with Willie).

CHAPTER SIX
1978

"Every Which Way But Loose" – Eddie Rabbit (1978)

Charlie Daniel's Volunteer Jam IV was aired live for the first time out of the Tennessee area when WHN broadcast the concert from Nashville's Municipal Auditorium on January 14th. The annual concert would mix country and rock performers playing together such as Black Oak Arkansas, the Outlaws, members of the Marshall Tucker Band with mainstream country artists like Willie Nelson, Tanya Tucker and Crystal Gayle. I attended so that someone would be on site to oversee the mix and the transmission and hang out with Charlie and the acts backstage. *Billboard* quoted me as saying, "We are pleased to broadcast the largest country music event in America on the world's largest country music station." It was also broadcast on WKDF, a Nashville rock station as usual. Charlie was quoted as appreciating the opportunity to reach the ten percent of the nation's population covered by WHN's signal. He was a great friend of WHN. He was another artist whose music was a big part of the evening show even when he was not releasing singles for country radio. Selections from that concert were released later in the year as the double album *Volunteer Jam III and IV* on Epic records.

Dr. Hook was a group formed in New Jersey whose principals were southerner Ray Sawyer (the one with the eye patch) and primary vocalist Jersey native Dennis Locorriere. Their "Sylvia's Mother," written by Shel Silverstein and covered for country radio by Bobby Bare, was a staple on Jessie's show. When they released "Only Sixteen" (a remake of the Sam Cooke hit), WHN jumped right on it. It was a huge WHN and pop hit. It earned a gold record, but only made the middle of the country charts. It was great to have another local artist on the station. Dr. Hook released other country flavored songs, "A Couple More Years"/"A Little Bit More" and then started to drift more into the pop sound with "Sharing The Night Together" and "When You're In Love With A Beautiful Woman." Ray and Dennis were very funny fellows and were very entertaining as guest deejays when they appeared on January 26th.

Another entertaining guest deejay was Billy Martin, the on again, off again manager of the New York Yankees. He was a WHN listener and played the station in the locker room. He had a reputation for being unpredictable, so I was on pins and needles whenever he went on the air. This year, Martin opened Billy Martin's Western Store at Madison Avenue and 69th Street. He said that his friend Mickey Mantle gave him the idea after Mantle took notice of a growing number of New Yorkers wearing cowboy boots. Martin's merchandise was not for the average WHN listener, or staff member. A pair of boots in his store could cost a lot more than the Gucci loafers we had considered a status symbol.

WHN did not choose sides between Yankees and Mets fans. New York Mets manager Joe Torre likewise appeared as guest deejay on WHN. It was customary for WHN to offer dinner at a restaurant to these sports stars as a gesture of thanks. I recall having to justify a particularly large dinner bill to management on one occasion when Torre invited some friends to join him. Even though the Yankees and Mets games were carried on other radio stations, appearances by their managers and players on WHN helped to reinforce the atmosphere of being a New York radio station.

WHN: WHEN NEW YORK CITY WENT COUNTRY

WHN did a live broadcast with Roy Head from the Lone Star Café on February 7th. Head was now recording country material for ABC/Dot, but had a pop and rhythm and blues hit with "Treat Her Right" in 1965. We had lunch that afternoon and he told some great stories about that era and our mutual friend, Huey Meaux, who had been his producer. Head had an exciting rock and roll act that included splits, flips and other contortions. He brought much of that charisma to his country act.

The Carpenters released "Sweet Sweet Smile," a song written by soon to be country star Juice Newton. It had such a country sound, WHN added it despite the pop image of the duo. Other country stations followed and the record actually became a bigger country hit than it was a pop hit for the Carpenters.

Rusty Weir did an in-studio concert at WHN on February 27th. Although Weir never had a hit country single, he was one of the album artists that WHN played in the evening as part of the station's "progressive country" repertoire. "Don't It Make You Wanna Dance" was a minor pop hit for him, but had been covered by, among others, Jerry Jeff Walker, Chris LeDoux and Barbara Mandrell. Bonnie Raitt's version of the song would make the country charts when it was included on the *Urban Cowboy* movie soundtrack.

"It's A Heartache" by Bonnie Tyler was another record that defied categorization. We tested it with listeners and they felt it belonged on WHN. Other country stations followed. This was certainly not a Nashville record; Tyler was from Wales. Country listeners embraced this song just as they had songs by English/Australian artist Olivia Newton-John. "It's A Heartache" became a top ten national country hit and an even bigger hit on Top 40 radio. I received a gold record award for breaking the record. Tyler said that after the success of this song on country radio, her producers insisted she aim for that market and record more country songs. However she considered herself a rock artist and refused. Tyler never had any more country hits in the US but in

1983 would top the pop charts with "Total Eclipse of the Heart" with another producer and record label.

British artist, Eric Clapton, released a song that did well on WHN, "Lay Down Sally." Since I was involved with KTNQ and WGBS, I was as familiar with the latest pop music as well as country and thought this would work on WHN. Because we had so much listener feedback through call out research and requests, I knew I would find out quickly if I was wrong and could pull the record. Country artist Red Sovine recorded a cover version, but WHN stuck with Clapton's record. Other country stations followed and "Lay Down Sally" by Eric Clapton became a top twenty country hit. It was a huge pop hit and a million seller, but RSO Records never sent me a gold record for breaking it country. They were a pop label and I don't think they cared about the country airplay, if they even noticed.

On the other end of the country spectrum, WHN broadcast a concert on May 10th with Country Music Hall of Famer Ernest Tubb from the Lone Star Café. Tubb was one of the biggest country stars of the 40s and 50s, but his last big hit was a 1969 duet with Loretta Lynn. He was out of fashion in this era of crossover country. It was almost airtime and Tubb was still on the bus and I went to get him. Mort Cooperman said, "Have a heart, don't you know he is a sick man?" Tubb was battling emphysema, which would take his life six years later. I was relieved when he emerged from the bus in the nick of time and seemed to draw energy from the appreciative audience. That show was memorialized in the First Generation Records CD *Ernest Tubb, Live From The Lone Star Café.*

That same month, WHN broadcast a live concert with Bill Anderson from Drew University in Madison, New Jersey. Anderson's country version of Orleans' "Still The One" had been a recent hit. Also on the bill was Mary Lou Turner, with whom Anderson had recorded a duet, as well was Hank Williams' Original Drifting Cowboys. The show was co-promoted by Richie

Allen Seinfeld, Freddie "The German Cowboy" Wenzler and Billy Wood.

Radio stations had an obligation to present public service programming in categories including religion. Like many stations, WHN satisfied this with hour or half hour shows programmed as a block on Sunday mornings and Sunday evenings. Public service director Jamie Wenner and I came up with a way to integrate religious programming into regular programming and eliminate the Sunday programs. She found a Catholic priest, a Protestant minister and a Jewish rabbi who were willing to write and read short religious reflections based on then popular WHN hits. She produced their commentaries packaged with the songs and they rotated through various weekday and weekend day parts.

I had gotten to know Billy Davis from the McCann Erickson advertising agency, which had produced Dottie West's "Country Sunshine." Davis served on the CMA Board of Directors, but had been a rhythm and blues singer, writer and producer and I had many of the records that he had been involved with in my collection. One day he called and asked if I would come in and do a voiceover for some Coca Cola commercials. It was a simple line, "Freddy Fender for Coca Cola." I didn't consider myself an announcer (I was one of the few program directors who had never been a disc jockey), so I declined. Davis insisted that I really should do it. Finally he agreed to my suggestion to have Mike Fitzgerald do the read. Several months later Mike came in to my office to thank me, as he had received his first check from the job. It was for $10,000. If I had known network television commercials paid that kind of money, I would have read that line forever until I did it to Davis' satisfaction.

Dan Abernathy was hired from WWL, New Orleans, as news director replacing Charlie Kaye. Abernathy was former group news director of Bartel Broadcasting (which owned WOKY Milwaukee, KCBQ San Diego, WDRQ Detroit, WMYQ Miami,

KSLQ St. Louis), and former news anchor/director of WXLO in New York, all Top 40 stations. WHN had cut back the news staff and I was looking for a way to compete with the far larger departments of our AM dial neighbor all news stations, WINS and WCBS. Abernathy had grown up in Detroit during the days when CKLW, a Top 40 music station licensed to Windsor, Canada, had the most entertaining and compelling news in the market and knew how deliver the news in a more concise and dramatic form than our competitors. He also had a passion for breaking news. For example, he wrote to his news staffers on August 3rd that WHN "led the City on every major news story of the day." Abernathy served as news director, street reporter and anchored news during morning drive.

In 1977, the movie *The Amityville Horror* came out about a Long Island murder. Dan Abernathy attempted to investigate it and met a ghost. Abernathy recalls, "Ronald DeFeo, Jr. shotgunned his mom, dad, sisters. He said that the house was haunted and the ghosts made him do it. This murder happened when I was at WXLO as news director. The Lutz family bought the house and wrote a book about the strange things that happened to them there and it was a best seller and also a big movie. Between the time that the book and movie came out the house was sold and the new owners moved in. Then the movie hit the big time. Suddenly people were showing up at the house demanding tours, parking in front of house at all house waiting to see ghosts. The new owners invited WHN to look to see that the story was all bull. I hadn't seen the movie yet, but I drove out there after my air shift. So I'm heading west and then start to head north to get to the George Washington Bridge to get home. I look down at my gas gauge and it is MOVING! It is moving from half full, to three quarter to full AND THEN IT MOVED RIGHT OFF THE DIAL and behind the cowling. I am quite concerned. Then it comes back down slowly to half full. I'm thinking 'Dan you've imagined that.' THEN IT DID IT AGAIN going just like the time before but then stays behind the cowling for much longer. I don't know if I should pull over and get out or what on the freeway. Then it stops and goes back to half full and stays there as I go north and then west to New Jersey. I've talked to ghost experts and they say that a poltergeist probably got in my car. The poltergeist didn't know how far I was going from his home so when I started going north this was where he was getting out and he pulled that stunt."

One of the biggest WHN hits this year came from a deejay at WLAC in Nashville, John Conlee. Although he was a deejay on a pop music station in Nashville, his "Rose Colored Glasses" was a huge country hit and he followed it with a string of hits that lasted more than a decade.

On July 17th, WHN received the New York State Broadcasters' Award for best promotional campaign in the state, from submissions by 287 stations. All of WHN's advertising was simple and consistent. It featured the most popular artists that the station played with the call letters and the dial position. The print ads usually had a slogan; the television ads had the artists talking about their music and saying, "ten-fifty, WHN."

New Yorker Paul Evans released another novelty song, "Hello, This Is Joannie," which featured the newly popular telephone answering machine in its lyrics. The song was a big WHN hit, and enough other country stations added it so that it reached the middle of the national country charts despite being on Spring Records, an independent label with no country connections whose biggest artist was rhythm and blues star Millie Jackson. It was a top ten pop hit in England and in other parts of the world, but did not make the US pop charts. Evans remembers, "it always seemed that (almost) every cab in New York at the time had the station on the car radio . . . and how many times did I hear 'Happy Birthday America' and 'Joannie' during a cab ride to or from a studio? Lots!" Evans told us when he went on vacation to Namibia in Africa, he found it had been a hit there as well. "I remember going back to Spring Records after a great tour of England and listen to them tell Jimmy Wisner, my great producer and I, that they had decided that I wouldn't be cutting 'country' anymore (They were basically an R&B label). Get me outta there! Jimmy did. And I remember that I thought Jimmy was going to jump across the table and clobber them when the owners gave us this information." Evans later wrote and recorded "Willie's Sung With Everyone But Me" listing Willie Nelson's duet partners. That song didn't motivate Nelson to sing with him, even though it was included on a CD release of Willie Nelson duets.

Tanya Tucker wrote and recorded "Save Me," a song to bring attention to the hunting of seals for fur, and brought it to the station for me to hear. After we had taken the normal publicity photos, someone (probably Harriet Sternberg, Tanya's publicist) suggested I put on a seal mask while Tanya hugged me protectively. That photo, captioned only "Radio exec Ed Salamon suffers mutely with Tanya," with no mention of the fact that I was wearing a mask, appeared in the July 13, 1978 issue of *Rolling Stone* magazine. Readers must have thought I was one weird looking person, giving a whole new meaning to the phrase "a face made for radio." It was to be the only time my photo ever appeared in *Rolling Stone*.

Meat Loaf had a million selling pop hit with "Two Out of Three Ain't Bad," a song that told a story as compelling as the country hits of the day. Epic recording artist Bobby Borchers must have felt likewise, as he began to perform the song in his live shows. I was well aware of the song because as national program director for Storer, I had added Meat Loaf's record at Top 40 10-Q radio in Los Angeles. Until that time, the record was considered an east coast hit, and I received a gold record for spreading it nationally. We began broadcasting shows live from the Palomino Club in North Hollywood on KGBS-FM. When Borchers did the song during his live broadcast, the audience went crazy. Pam Green, who was vacationing in LA, happened to be there as well. We looked at each other and knew that song had to be on the radio. We began airing it on KGBS-FM and Green took it back and added it at WHN. We sent copies to Epic and to the song's publisher. The publisher sent it to a number of other country stations, who played it from the tape. I recall it at No. 3 on the WHK, Cleveland charts. Epic was not happy, because they felt that it was competing with Borchers' official release. Since it wasn't a record, it never charted nationally, despite high chart positions at some significant country radio stations. I understand Epic tried to record a studio version, but were not satisfied with it. Famed producer Jimmy Bowen, with a rival label, heard the live recording and said they should have released the live recording as it was. That was only one of many concert recordings that WHN excerpted from live broadcasts whch were played on the air. These days, I hear Nashville's AM country station, WSM, playing live recordings from the Grand Ole Opry on the air. At the time, I'm not aware of any other country stations that did that, except for our sister station KGBS-FM.

Alan Colmes was doing a stand-up comedy act at the time and had a booking at a prestigious venue and invited me to attend. In one of his bits, he spoofed his work on WHN and some of the listeners who called him. Afterwards, I went backstage and he asked me what I thought. I told him if he ever did that WHN bit again, he would no longer be able to work at the station. Colmes is also author of the book *Red, White and Liberal*, which he signed to me, "I don't know where I'd be if it wasn't for you."

WHN helped establish Big Al Downing, who became the second most successful black artist in country music at that time. Tony Bongiovi and Lance Quinn from the Power Station, a New York recording studio, had produced some recordings with Downing. I had frequented the studio when Robert Gordon was recording there and had met Tony and Lance. I probably also met Tony's nephew Jon, who was helping around the studio at the time, but don't recall meeting him until he was better known as Jon Bon Jovi. I was there when artists including David Bowie were recording; it was a hot studio at the time. When I heard the tracks, I was surprised. I owned Al's previous rock and roll records "Down On The Farm," "Oh Babe" and "Georgia Slop" which were played at teen dances when I was in high school. Now he was a convincing country singer with songs he wrote himself. His first single, "Mr. Jones," was a huge request. It became No. 1 on WHN and top twenty on the national country charts. His follow up hits "Touch Me (I'll Be Your Fool Once More)" and "Bring It On Home" did just as well nationally. Al and I became friend. I accompanied him when he performed at the Grand Ole Opry and he asked me to write the liner notes for a retrospective of his country material.

Delbert McClinton's music was hard to categorize. Country, blues and rock and roll all influenced his work. Although he had no hit singles, he was one of the artists that Jessie played regularly in the evenings. His new single, "Giving It Up For Your Love" was climbing the pop, but not country charts. Nevertheless, WHN was playing it and were glad to have the opportunity to broadcast his concert at the Lone Star Café on July 25th. It was not unusual for celebrities to be in the audience of our live broadcasts. That evening, Elvis Costello, a big McClinton fan, was in the audience. Costello jumped up on stage during McClinton's set to sing with him and Delbert blurted out "Holy shit, its Elvis Costello." I was in the audience and therefore couldn't know whether our engineer had caught the expletive and used the delay button so it would not go out over the air. Lone Star manager Mort Cooperman offered to make sure Delbert was aware that we were on live radio. He quickly scribbled a note and handed it to Delbert. Delbert looked at it and said. "Oh fuck, I just got a note saying I can't say shit on the radio." At that point our engineer made the decision to terminate the broadcast. WHN listeners never got the opportunity to hear any more of the amazing McClinton and Costello performance. *Rolling Stone* magazine covered the concert in their Random Notes column in their next issue, and I got a nice apology note from Delbert.

Lee Arnold recalls another memorable concert at the Lone Star Café, this one with Larry Gatlin; "As success started to happen with his record career, it was a hard thing to handle for Larry. That was when his battles with the demons began. It took the form of drugs and alcohol. During that period, I did not suspect a thing. He covered up pretty well. What perplexed me is how rude he was to fans. I thought it was ego and he was just being temperamental. One night after introducing him at the Lone Star Café, he began singing and in the middle of one of his songs he turned to a couple sitting ringside and started to berate them 'I came here to sing; you came here to listen. If you don't shut up then get the hell out of here.' Not exactly the way to win friends and influence people." Gatlin was quoted by *People* magazine: "Five dollars don't entitle a fan to come in and ruin our shows."

Dr. Norman Vincent Peale, the author of *The Power of Positive Thinking*, purchased time each Sunday morning for his radio show to run on WHN. It was the successor to his *Art of Living*, which had been broadcast on the NBC radio network. I was hired by Dr. Peale to work on the show as a side project. He would record his sermons at the Marble Collegiate Church each week. The sermons varied in length and needed to be separated so commercials could be inserted. I would edit them and then write the necessary transitions as well as an introduction and a reflection on the sermon so that it would time out to a half hour *Power Of Positive Thinking* radio show. Mike Fitzgerald read the script. The production was done at Narwood Productions in midtown Manhattan, a few blocks away from WHN. Sometimes I was asked to write additional continuity for Dr. Peale himself to read and I would coach him through the script. I was flattered that I captured his sentiments so well that he never made any changes to what I had written, either for Mike or for himself. At the time, I did not know about Dr. Peale's one time prejudice against Catholics, as displayed in his campaign against John F. Kennedy's election. Likewise, he did not know I was a Catholic. It never came up.

In August, WHN won more *Billboard* awards than any other radio station that year. *Billboard* magazine named WHN Country Station of the Year. Larry Kenney was named Country Air Personality of the Year and I was named Country Program Director of the Year. One of my 10-Q deejays, Machine Gun Kelly, won the award as Rock Personality of the Year. The awards were presented at *Billboard's* Radio Forum held in New York. Dale Pon, now director of creative services for Storer Radio, spoke at the convention about how promotion affects ratings. I spoke on the panel "Where Will They Come From" about developing leadership in the industry.

About this time the program director of WIRE in Indianapolis, Gary Havens, remembers visiting WHN. We always liked to show visiting radio folks the station. Havens recalls being most impressed by the way WHN prepared the music logs for the air personalities. WHN used a metal form with title strips, which was the way many stations prepared their commercial logs in the days before computers. The frames were then copied. Havens says "I followed the work you pioneered in music testing and attempted to recreate that at WIRE. We used RAM research and Jack McCoy to do call outs. The idea that the program director and not the jock would make the song-by-song music decisions based on research from listeners was a big change. I always thought WHN set the standard and led the way in that." Havens would become program director of WHN in 1986.

Wink Martindale's "Deck Of Cards" had remained as one of the more than 2,000 records in WHN's oldies rotation because of consistent listener requests. However, the record really annoyed

Neil Rockoff every time he heard it. In October he sent me a note saying, "'Deck Of Cards' gets tossed—no democratic decision on that one." We pulled it from the library.

Ronnie Milsap played the Bottom Line in September. There were special t-shirts made up for this appearance; country acts still considered playing the Bottom Line as quite a coup. Milsap was in the middle of a long string of No. 1 country hits, and the previous year, his "Almost like A Song" had crossed over and became a pop hit. Milsap again sat in as a guest deejay and, as had become our custom, we had a Braille transcriber on hand so that he was able to read weather, traffic, promos and commercials.

That fall Storer announced that they were beginning to sell off their radio stations to invest in cable television. There was no more need for me to spend so much time in Los Angeles, so I returned to WHN where I still held the program director title. In recognition for the outstanding job Charlie Cook had done as acting program director of WHN during my absence, I proposed that he become program director of Storer's WCBS in Miami. He accepted. Robbie Roman returned to WHN as assistant program director. Dene Hallam had replaced Roman as program director of KBZT (K-Best) in San Diego shortly before that station went on the air in September.

Susan Storms Schlosser joined the station, initially as the programming department secretary. She had escaped from Iran, where she had been teaching English to the Shah's children, just before he was overthrown in an Islamic revolution and replaced by the Ayatollah Khomeini. She proved just as resourceful at WHN and grew into a highly successful press and public relations professional.

"It's A Heartache" by Bonnie Tyler wound up as the No. 1 song that year for WHN. Artists having more than a couple of songs on the 1978 WHN Top 105 year end chart included Kenny Rogers, Dolly Parton, the Oak Ridge Boys, Willie Nelson and Waylon Jennings.

```
                                  Jan. 29,'77

    Dear Neil:

    Thank you very much for the Male
    Vocalist and Entertainer of the
    Year awards from the WHN poll. I
    really do appreciate the loyal
    support of so many fans as were
    part of your listener project---
    and your thoughtful note. Best
    wishes always and may God bless
    you all.           Sincerely,
```

Elvis Presley so appreciated being voted Male Vocalist and Entertainer of the Year in WHN's Listener's Choice Awards, that he sent a thank you card to general manager Neil Rockoff. Elvis also had his WHN awards hung along side of his earliest gold records in his Trophy Room, where they still hang today.

WHN ran this advertisement in industry trade magazines promoting its consistent position near the top of the New York radio market.

On Wednesday, May 25th, 1977 WHN air personalities participated in a "WHN Night At The Meadowlands" promotion at that New Jersey racetrack. Del De Montreux holds the reins and Ed Salamon presents him with a trophy as Ed Baer, Lee Arnold and Bob Wayne look on. The four air personalities raced against each other driving sulky carts pulled by horses.

Charlie Daniels made one of his frequent appearances as a WHN guest deejay in 1977. Front row: Ed Salamon, Pam Green, Daniels, Del De Montreux. Back row: Jessie, Bob Wayne, Peter Kanze, Charlie Cook. (Courtesy Peter Kanze)

Olivia Newton-John often visited WHN during her string of pop/country crossover records. Here she is shown in 1977 with Ed Salamon, vice president general manager Neil Rockoff and creative services director Dale Pon.

Emmylou Harris (center) is shown in the WHN lobby with Charlie Cook and Bob Wayne after appearing as a gust deejay during Wayne's show.

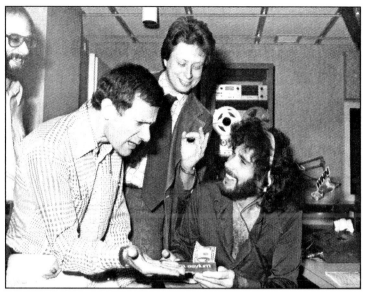

Lee Arnold pretends to demand payola from New Jersey native Eddie Rabbitt who hands over his latest single and a twenty dollar bill during a 1977 visit, while Ed Salamon gestures approvingly and Charlie Cook looks on. Rabbitt had an unbroken string of top ten records for more than a dozen years.

WHN's 1977 ad campaign, created by Dale Pon, used the slogan "WHN gives you music you wanna hear" rather than promote the station as country. Trade publications reported it as the first authorized use of Elvis Presley's name and likeness to endorse a radio station. An accompanying television spot utilized archive press conference film of Elvis. Artists in this campaign included Kenny Rogers, Johnny Cash and Linda Ronstadt, among others.

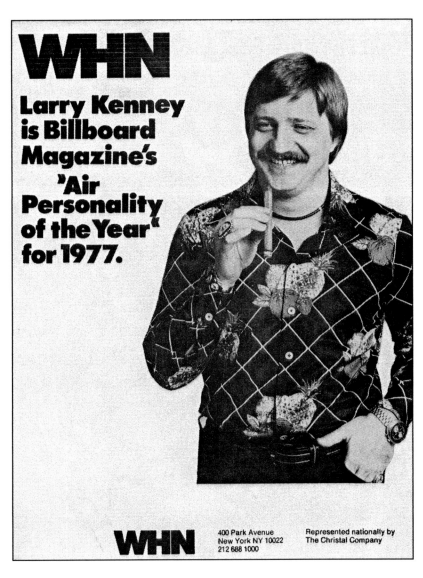

Larry Kenney, a gifted voice artist and humorist, had joined WHN in 1974 and was morning air personality from 1975 until 1979. He was named 1977 *Billboard* magazine Air Personality of the Year.

Backstage at a WHN live broadcast of a Bill Anderson concert in May 1978 at Drew University in Madison, New Jersey are (front row) Billy Wood (promoter), Art Mahr, (*Country Music* magazine), Freddie "The German Cowboy" Wenzler (promoter), Joseph Stuart (producer *One Life to Live* TV show); (second row) Richie Allen (promoter), Mary Lou Turner, Del De Montreux, Jill Voit (*One Life To Live* cast); (row three) Alan Furst (WBAX Program Director), Dean McNett, Bob McNett, Hillous Buttram, Jerry Rivers, Don Helms (all Hank Williams' Original Drifting Cowboys), Bill Anderson; (row four) Pam Green, Ed Salamon.

Baseball greats Joe Torre and Tommy Lasorda sat in as guest deejays at WHN in 1978. Standing are Del De Montreux with Torre, then NY Mets manager, and WHN sports director Howie Rose. Seated are Lasorda, then LA Dodgers manager and Ed Salamon. (Courtesy Howie Rose)

On March 10, 1979 James Brown performed at the Grand Ole Opry as the guest of Porter Wagoner. Ed Salamon was in Nashville attending the Country Radio Seminar and went to see the show with *Radio and Records* country editor Jim Duncan. Afterwards Salamon hung out with Brown and Wagoner in Brown's dressing room.

How Does A Radio Station Make A Face Familiar?

"There goes Bloomingdale's."

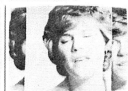

New Yorkers got to know Anne Murray's face through WHN's ads.

New Yorkers get to know advertisers with help from WHN.

Every night television viewers in the metropolitan area meet their favorite **WHN** stars. And while the stars chat about themselves and sing their songs in **WHN** commercials, the viewers get to know them. Sometimes a little too well.

Anne Murray learned that recently. We all know Anne, right? Years of great, beautiful songs. A fresh look nobody could miss, no matter how big the crowd.

Well, it's not entirely so. While Anne's had giant hits, she could still drop into

New York from Toronto and shop without anyone recognizing her.

That is, until Anne began appearing on TV to say "1050 **WHN**." On her last trip, cab drivers knew her instantly. So did people in New York's most fashionable stores. Suddenly, an anonymous shopper was a traffic stopper. Which prompted Anne to report, at the end of a private little jaunt that turned very public, "There goes Bloomingdale's."

You may not be finding Anne Murray in Bloomies much anymore, but you will find

WHN listeners. The fact is that through **WHN**'s ad campaigns we're making 1,000,000,000 impressions.

People who are learning about **WHN**, tuning to it, and staying with the station. The same way they return again and again to stores they know and styles they love.

We made Anne Murray's face familiar. We can help do the same for advertisers, too.

By playing the music listeners want to hear, **WHN** gives you the people you want to reach.

After Anne Murray appeared in television ads for WHN, she said that she could no longer walk around New York unrecognized. WHN's television and subway campaigns, which associated the station with some of the biggest artists of the era, including Murray, Kenny Rogers, Linda Ronstadt, the Eagles, and Elvis Presley, made more than one billion impressions on New Yorkers.

R&B star Millie Jackson was a WHN listener and recorded versions of songs she heard on the station, including Merle Haggard's "If We're Not Back In Love By Monday". Jackson worked up a special set of all country material for a WHN live concert broadcast from the Lone Star Café. Ed Salamon is shown with Jackson backstage at that event.

Kenny Rogers and WHN swapped awards in 1979, when Rogers received four WHN Listeners' Choice awards for solo recording and duets with Dottie West. Ed Salamon received gold album awards for *The Gambler* and *Classics* (Rogers' duet album with West). Shown are United Artists promotion manager Milt Allen, WHN vice president general manger Nick Verbitsky, Rogers, Pam Green and Salamon.

On September 24th, 1979 Moe Bandy and Joe Stampley, who were recording as the duet Moe and Joe, stopped by WHN to be guest deejays and, while there, helped celebrate Alan Colmes' birthday.

WHN's 1979 ad campaign featured the slogan "Your Heart's In The Right Place", with no mention of country. This ad was designed by Mark Larson under the supervision of WHN creative services director Fred Siebert. Kenny Rogers was featured along with Elvis Presley, Dolly Parton, Olivia Newton-John, and Anne Murray.

John Hartford appeared on Jessie's show as a guest deejay, and also performed live. Hartford insisted WHN provide a sheet of plywood so that he could dance on it during his performance.

In 1980, Mickey Gilley visited New York for a WHN broadcast from the Lone Star Café, performing songs that would be in *The Urban Cowboy*. WHN arranged to welcome him on the Spectacolor sign in Times Square. Ed Salamon took Gilley to see the sign.

CHAPTER SEVEN
1979

"Pilot of the Airwaves" – Charlie Dore (1979)

In January, to celebrate Elvis Presley's birthday, WHN had listeners vote for their favorite fifty Elvis songs and compiled a list of WHN listeners' "50 All-Time Elvis Presley Favorites," which we featured on a countdown. The top five vote getters were "Love Me Tender," "My Way," "Hound Dog," "Teddy Bear" and "Can't Help Falling In Love."

The Dukes of Hazzard debuted as a mid season replacement on the CBS television network. The country themed show starred both John Schneider, who played Bo Duke, and Tom Wopat, who played Luke Duke. Both John, who was from the New York area and a WHN listener, and Tom became good friends of the station and appeared a number of times as guest deejays. Waylon Jennings performed the theme, which became a big WHN hit, and served as an off-camera narrator for the show. In its second season, the show began to incorporate guest appearances by WHN artists including Hoyt Axton, Donna Fargo, Freddy Fender, the Oak Ridge Boys, Roy Orbison, Buck Owens, Mickey Gilley and Dottie West, among others. *The Dukes of Hazzard* lasted on CBS through 1985 and then continued as reruns in off-network syndication.

In February, *Billboard* reported a live broadcast that WHN

aired with Texas artist Steve Fromholtz from the Lone Star Café on January 26th, noting by that time the station had done over one hundred broadcasts from various New York venues. Fromholz wrote "I'd Have To Be Crazy," which had been a recent hit by Willie Nelson. That same month, WHN began broadcasting the best of its live concerts every Sunday evening. WHN production director Ron Schiller edited the tapes of the original broadcast air checks.

On March 10th, I was in Nashville for the 10th annual Country Radio Seminar, where I spoke on a panel on ratings and research. After the panels concluded, Jim Duncan, who was the country editor of *Radio and Records*, and I drove from the downtown hotel where the convention was being held to see the Grand Ole Opry at the Opry House near Opryland. Porter Wagoner had invited James Brown to perform that evening. Brown performed "Tennessee Waltz" and some other country standards, which were warmly received, and then went into "Papa's Got A Brand New Bag," at which point he lost the audience. I've heard accounts of the evening reporting it as racial bias, but that is not what happened. The audience was made up of country music lovers and as long as Brown sang that genre, he was accepted. The crowd was not rhythm and blues or rock and roll fans and they reacted negatively when he performed that material.

In March, Willie Nelson was in New York for a live NBC television special and he was a guest deejay during Lee Arnold's show. Like Waylon Jennings, Bill Anderson, Tom T. Hall and John Conlee, Nelson had worked as a deejay in Texas when he was starting his music career. Except for his distinctive voice, when he sat in as guest deejay it didn't sound all that different from the regular format.

That same month, Kenny Rogers sat in as a guest deejay on Mike Fitzgerald's afternoon show. Rogers was in town for his first show at Carnegie Hall on March 22nd. Dottie West, who appeared on the show with Kenny, likewise was a guest deejay.

The Oak Ridge Boys were also on that show. There was an after party at Regine's and I recall spending time that evening talking with WHN listener Harry Reasoner, founder of CBS television's *60 Minutes*, who was back with that show after a stint with ABC, where he co-anchored the *ABC Evening News*.

In April, RCA representative Tim McFadden brought Tom T. Hall to WHN to sit in as guest deejay during Lee Arnold's show. Hall had also worked as a disc jockey on Armed Forces Radio and at WMOR, Moorhead, Kentucky, so he was pretty good at it. He had a number of songs in WHN's library, notably "I Love" which had crossed from country to pop radio a few years earlier. Hall had just written a book *How I Write Songs*.

In April, I met Dick Clark for the first time. He visited WHN and agreed to be a guest deejay to promote the *Academy of Country Music Awards* television show which he produced. He sat in during Del De Montreux's afternoon show. Dick began his broadcast career in Syracuse, New York, where he once did a country music show as "Cactus Dick." Since I grew up watching *American Bandstand*, I was a fan and asked him to sign an album, which he did graciously. I then asked him to sign a second album. Even in the days before autographed items were being sold on eBay, I believe he must have thought I was taking advantage of the situation and wrote on it "Get a good price for this one, Ed." Today that's probably my favorite autographed item.

Michael Martin Murphey made his second appearance as a WHN guest deejay on Jessie's show. Murphey was in town for Country Comes To Carnegie Hall on May 30th. The show also featured Tammy Wynette and Johnny Rodriguez.

Buck Owens was a guest deejay on June 15th. Afterwards we had a long conversation over drinks at a bar near the United Nations. Not one to pull any punches, Owens told me that he meant every word of his 1970 hit "I Wouldn't Live in New York City (If They Gave Me The Whole Dang Town)." He sympathized with me about the flack WHN received from the Nashville country music community. Buck felt that, being California based, the country music establishment had been somewhat inhospitable to him, favoring artists based in Nashville. Like WHN, he was accused of being "not country enough" when his record, "Tiger By The Tail," became a Top 40 radio hit. In addition to being one of country music's all time most successful artists, and an influence on pop groups including the Beatles, Owens was also a successful businessman, owning radio stations in Phoenix and Bakersfield.

This year Dr. Jerry Carroll joined WHN for weekends and fill-in. Carroll had most recently been afternoons on Top 40 WPIX-FM, but was better known for his role playing a frenetic nonstop salesman in commercials for the Crazy Eddie electronics chain.

Linda Ronstadt released a version of the Elvis Presley classic "Love Me Tender." We decided to edit her version together with Elvis' original to make a WHN exclusive duet. That exclusive version received a lot of airplay on the station and was a big request item with listeners, who could not buy it or hear it anywhere else. Because the singers recorded for different record labels, it would have been impossible for the labels themselves to create the duet. Neither of the labels complained, and WHN had an exclusive hit.

RCA released the album *Rock Billy Boogie* by Robert Gordon. Robert had moved to New York from the Washington D.C. area, and became a favorite of Bruce Springsteen, who wrote the song "Fire," later a hit for the Pointer Sisters, for him. Gordon had also been lead singer of the Tuff Darts, a band I had seen at CBGBs, but his heart was in rockabilly rather than punk music. Gordon had become a regular performer at the Lone Star Café, and we did a number of live broadcasts with him. Songs from which were later compiled into the *Live At Lone Star* album. Two singles from the *Rock Billy Boogie* album, "It's Only Make Believe" and "Walk On By" were big hits on WHN and both made the national country charts as a result, although the label did not promote them to country radio. Robert loved the 50s and really lived the part. When I visited him in his West Side apartment, the décor was mid-century down to vintage beverage glasses. Robert was a real country fan and recalls, "I've met a lot of artists, but when I went to Nashville to record with the vocal group The Nashville Edition, I got to meet Faron Young, who was recording in the next studio. 'Hello Walls' was one of my favorite records and when I shook his hand it was like an electric shock." When Michael Martin Murphey was interviewed in *Variety* in June about the changes in country music, he cited WHN and Gordon as an example: "WHN N.Y. is more progressive that way. They'll play Robert Gordon. But country fans always liked rockabilly, like Elvis Presley and Chuck Berry." I introduced Gordon to Dorsey Burnette, who had written "Rock Billy Boogie" with his brother Johnny in the 50s, and was recording country material at this time. Burnette died suddenly of a heart attack on August 19th. A few days later, I received a package from him in the mail. It was postmarked the day he died and contained an album of his early rock and roll recordings, as The Rock and Roll Trio.

In May, RCA promo representative Tim McFadden brought Chet Atkins to the station to be guest deejay before Atkins' appearance at Carnegie Hall. Freddy Fender did a live WHN broadcast from the Lone Star Café and sat in as a guest deejay during Del De Montreux's show.

That same month, WHN presented a week long series of live concert broadcasts. They included Johnny Paycheck at the Lone Star Café, Emmylou Harris from the Calderone Theater in Hempstead, Long Island, Hank Thompson from Cooper Union Hall in Greenwich Village, Vassar Clements at the Lone Star Café and Tammy Wynette, Johnny Rodriguez and Michael Martin Murphey at Carnegie Hall. The May 30th Carnegie Hall show was also simulcast on WPLO (Atlanta), WDGY (Minneapolis),

KENR (Houston), WDAF (Kansas City) and KMPS (Seattle). Lee Arnold was master of ceremonies and Mike Fitzgerald handled backstage commentary.

In June, WHN received a duet record from RCA by Jim Reeves and Deborah Allen, "Don't Let Me Cross Over." Reeves had died in a plane crash in 1964, and Allen was a new RCA artist. This duet was similar to what WHN had done with the Elvis and Linda Ronstadt's "Love Me Tender" earlier this year. Deborah Allen would have the unique distinction of having three duets with a dead man become top ten national hits. She certainly gave a new meaning to the phrase "resurrecting a career." Deborah and Pam Green became good friends and we got to spend time with Deborah's then husband, songwriter Rafe Van Hoy and their friend David Keith, who would star in the movie *An Officer and A Gentleman*. A few years later, Deborah would have a crossover hit with a song she wrote "Baby I Lied" which would be a top ten country and adult contemporary hit and reach the twenties on the national pop charts.

London's *Financial Times* June 11th edition carried an article about the growth of country which said, "New York's country station, WHN, is a good example of the growing bounds of country music."

Madison Avenue magazine ran a featured story on Nick Verbitsky and featured Nick, Dale and me in the article's photo. The article was captioned "Can country make it in the city? WHN's No. 2 position and $14 million price tag are proof positive." The $14 million referred to an "agreement in principal" that Storer had with Mutual Broadcasting Systems. WHN's press reprint highlighted a quote from the article: "WHN success comes from a combination of persistent salesmanship, skillful marketing and, of course, good programming."

When broadcasting in a major entertainment center like New York, you never know what celebrity might be listening to your station. It turned out that rhythm and blues star Millie Jackson was a regular WHN listener and in fact had used WHN for material. She had become fond of the music she heard on WHN and had recorded her own version of Merle Haggard's "If We're Not Back In Love By Monday" (as "If You're Not Back In Love By Monday") and Kenny Rogers' "Sweet Music Man." Both songs were substantial rhythm and blues radio hits and windfall royalties for those two country artists, who happened to write those songs. She later would record additional country songs, including the Don Gibson standard "I Can't Stop Loving You." Jackson worked up an entire country show for a live concert broadcast at the Lone Star Café. Her regular shows contained adult material, but she did a family friendly show at the Lone Star that night. On the recording that exists of the broadcast, she can be heard reassuring me that it would be a clean show, despite requests from some in the audience for her raunchy material. Jackson told me that she was exposed to country music as a child when her very religious parents only allowed her to watch *The Tennessee Ernie Ford Show* on television, because it contained hymns.

Pam Green recalls, "There were so many parties and concert broadcasts from the Lone Star. I wonder how I remember them because I enjoyed my share of Texas Tornados—a specialty drink served in a mason jar. Ed Salamon pushed the envelope in selecting artists for our broadcasts with Levon Helm, Millie Jackson and others. It was so unusual to have a stage facing the bar. Tables were on the sides so you could hardly see the stage. The best seats were upstairs where you overlooked the bar. I remember attending several *Saturday Night Live* after parties at the Lone Star. Years later I was talking to original SNL member Jane Curtin and she told me that she lived pretty close to the club. When the Lone Star moved to West 52nd Street, it just wasn't the same."

Many times Mort Cooperman would call me late on a Saturday night to tell me when artists would be performing there at

4:00 am after the club closed. I recall seeing the Blues Brothers and Willie Nelson among others, and going into Manhattan for the Rolling Stones, but they never showed.

At the end of his contract, Larry Kenney was replaced in mornings by Del De Montreux. Although Del didn't do voice impressions or character bits like Larry did, he gave the market a "more music in the morning" alternative to other stations that packed that part of the day with information and features. I'll always remember Del's time checks, as he reported the time "on the schnozz." Larry joined WYNY, an adult contemporary station, three months later.

New Yorker Rupert Holmes released "Escape (The Pina Colada Song)" and we felt that it was worth testing with our listeners. Perhaps they identified with the similar feel as Jimmy Buffett's "Margaritaville," but they felt the song fit our station, and WHN had another local artist to champion. Rupert wrote me that: "I hear myself with the likes of Tom T. Hall and Crystal Gayle and I am thrilled beyond belief." I thought of that letter years later when I read a comment by the Dixie Chicks that they didn't want their music played next to that of Reba McEntire and how different these artists' attitudes were. Although "Escape" did well on WHN, other country stations did not follow on this, but it did become a No. 1 pop hit and earned a gold record.

Lionel Richie and the Commodores' country sounding "Sail On" was also played on WHN this year. Unfortunately, it didn't do well enough for other country stations to pick it up, so it never made the national country charts. It did give Richie his first country airplay. In 1980, Richie would write and produce "Lady" for Kenny Rogers, which became a No. 1 country hit. In 2012, Richie would release his own first project actually aimed at country radio, *Tuskegee*, a duet album with established country artists. He probably didn't even realize that his first country radio exposure was twenty years earlier.

Charlie Daniels released "The Devil Went Down To Georgia," which became both a pop and country hit and a platinum single. Daniels brought his guitar to Jessie's show and played a live set of music. Daniels recalls, "Whenever I did that I could sing songs I hadn't recorded. I might even sing a Willie Nelson song. It was a big deal for me to do that." Daniels came to the station whenever he was in New York to sit in as a guest deejay or perform. "You might say I was a regular there."

Many credit Randy Travis with the "new traditional" movement in country music, which was young artists performing in an older style. But before Randy came along in the early 80s, John Anderson was blazing the same trail. His "Your Lying Blue Eyes" became a WHN listener favorite this year.

Rosanne Cash, Johnny's daughter, released a duet with Bobby Bare "No Memories Hangin' Round," which became a national country hit. She followed up with a string of solo hits. At the time she was married to Rodney Crowell and once when I was in Nashville they invited me to their home. As someone used to New York and LA, I was impressed that they could live on a secluded wooded lot and still be so close to Nashville. I remarked that one could go around naked out here and Rodney said that they sometimes did. Whenever possible, I like to look at the record collections of the folks I visit. Rosanne and Rodney's were on shelves in the dining room. I was surprised that there were so many classical records. Rosanne said she played them during mealtimes to calm their kids.

In July, the St. James Theater presented Broadway Opry '79. Forty-five acts in fifteen separate programs were scheduled to appear, including Ronnie Milsap, Conway Twitty and the Bellamy Brothers. WHN had negotiated to broadcast all of the shows. The series was intended to run for five weeks, but closed after the second week. The first shows were headlined by Waylon Jennings. The second week's shows did not do as well and the producers dropped the ticket price. Some shows had to be called off when a headliner cancelled his appearance. Don Gibson was among the artists who visited WHN to promote the series by being a guest deejay.

That same month, WHN also broadcast concerts from the Princeton Country Music Festival in New Jersey. Artists appearing included Roy Clark, the Oak Ridge Boys, Larry Gatlin and Con Hunley. That month, WHN Lone Star Café concert broadcasts included Hank Williams, Jr. and the Bellamy Brothers.

Although the Bottom Line presented a fair share of country artists, WHN seldom did live broadcasts from there. Progressive rock station WNEW had right of first refusal and would air concerts by Linda Ronstadt, Charlie Daniels and other artists that might have been more appropriate on WHN. WHN did get permission to broadcast a George Jones concert which WNEW had passed on. Unfortunately, George was living up to his "no show" nickname at that time and crawled out the bathroom window in the Bottom Line to avoid his handlers and the performance. The following year, Jones did show and both Linda Ronstadt and Bonnie Raitt surprised the crowd to sing duets with him.

In August, Larry and Rudy Gatlin were in New York for a meeting with the Gatlin Brothers' new label, Columbia Records, and sat in as guest deejays during Mike Fitzgerald's show.

The *New York Daily News* reported that WHN marked the second anniversary of Elvis Presley's death with a special program. The show included recollections of Elvis by B. J. Thomas, Tanya Tucker, Larry Gatlin and Bill Anderson, among others.

In September, Dale Pon left WHN to head creative services at WNBC, where Bob Pittman was program director. WNBC was challenging WABC and when identifying the station, they would always over accentuate the "N" in WNBC, presumably to distinguish it from its direct competitor.

WHN ran a subway campaign featuring Dolly Parton, Elvis Presley, Crystal Gayle, Anne Murray, Olivia Newton-John and Kenny Rogers with the slogan "Your Heart's In The Right Place."

Anne Murray appeared as a WHN guest deejay during Mike Fitzgerald's show before her concert at Carnegie Hall in September. That same month Fitzgerald played shortstop as one of the "Mets All Stars" in a pre-game exhibition. His team won.

The national radio show *Live From The Lone Star Café* debuted that fall. Radio syndicator Clayton Webster syndicated performances taped at the club for a weekly show. The first show in the series featured Moe Bandy and Joe Stampley, who were hot on the charts with their duet "Just Good Ol' Boys." Other mainstream country artists in the series included Mickey Gilley, Freddy Fender and Hank Williams, Jr. In keeping with the eclectic nature of the club and of WHN live broadcasts, artists including Jerry Jeff Walker, Asleep At The Wheel and New Riders of the Purple Sage were also featured. The series ran until the end of the following year. By that time the Lone Star Café was packed due to the influx of people visiting New York from other cities who had heard of the club on their local country radio station airing the show.

The September 15th edition of *Cash Box* carried an entire section devoted to WHN, which the trade magazine called "simply the most talked-about radio station in the entire New York area." One of the articles noted that WHN advertisers now included Firestone, Carvel, Heineken Beer, the Dime Savings Bank of New York, Chevrolet, TWA, American Airlines, Air France, Perrier and Blue Nun Wine. Another noted, "Salamon is controversial because his methodology has changed the face and texture of country music programming." It also noted that "Col. Tom Parker, Presley's manager, has authorized WHN as the only radio station in the country to use Presley's photo along with his signature as part of WHN promotions."

On September 24th, Moe Bandy and Joe Stampley, who were recording as the duet Moe and Joe, stopped by WHN to be guest deejays and, while there, helped celebrate Alan Colmes' birthday. Colmes recalls, "I worked my way up from a once-a-week Sunday shift to filling in on the overnights when the talent went on vacation and overnight man Ed Baer would sit in for them. And every once-in-a-while I even got to fill a prime time shift during the week. Country artists loved appearing on the station as guest DJ's and during one of my stints Moe and Joe, Moe Bandy and Joe Stampley, presented me with a cake and sang happy birthday to me. One of the desk assistants joked that with me there, it was now 'Moe, Joe and Schmo.' No matter. For a kid who grew up on Long Island and whose goal in life was to be on New York radio, this was a big deal. It was my entrée to the big time."

The September 29th issue of *Record World* featured me along with WNBC's Bob Pittman, WBLS's Frankie Crocker, WPLJ's Larry Berger and others in a feature "New York Radio; The Big Apple's Still The Biggest Challenge." *Record World* noted, "WHN has long since silenced those who believed a modern country format could never take hold in New York." With WHN proving the viability of country radio in what had been considered the most unlikely market, more and more stations changed format to full time country. Notably WSM in Nashville, known for carrying the *Grand Ole Opry*, switched from adult contemporary music to country this month.

Pope Paul II arrived in New York on October 2nd. Dan Abernathy remembers, "On the parade for the Pope, I was walking inside the police line with my microphone sign that said WHN just ahead of the Pope and people were cheering me and saying 'HEY, THERE'S WHN!!!'"

The October 13th issue of *Billboard* included a country section which noted that WHN had reported the highest listener ratings ever this year. *Billboard's* Ed Morris called WHN's playlist "a model, both in scope and flexibility."

In October, Kenny Rogers presented WHN with gold records for the albums *The Gambler* and *Classics* (with Dottie West).

At the same event, WHN presented Kenny Rogers with awards from the 4th annual WHN Listeners' Choice Awards for Entertainer of the Year, Single of the Year and Group or Duo of the Year (with Dottie West).

Each year when daylight savings time came to an end the clocks were turned back by an hour. That meant the overnight show would be extended by an hour. For a number of years, Ed Baer had been calling in sick at the last minute on that night. The part time air talent had noticed and pointed it out to me and other WHN management, and made us feel bad that we permitted it. Sure enough, that weekend Ed called in sick again. Maybe it was the extra hour, or maybe it was just Baer's way of expressing frustration for not being promoted into a daytime time slot. I felt that Baer never sounded the way I wanted the station to sound, but he was fine in the overnight time slot where he was when I arrived. We decided to make a change and hired Dan Taylor, who was doing overnights at WCBS-FM. He would be the second consecutive WCBS-FM overnight air personality that I had hired. Baer went on to work at Adult Contemporary formatted WYNY and later had a long run doing the morning show at WHUD in Peekskill.

The first Reba McEntire record that I recall WHN playing was "Sweet Dreams," a former Patsy Cline hit written by Don Gibson. Reba had been recording with Mercury records for about three years at that time and country music listeners are lucky that they stuck with her. For many years she closed her show with an acappella version of that song. At this writing, McEntire holds the record for the most Academy of Country Music Top Female Vocalist Awards (seven) and ties with Martina McBride for most Country Music Association Female Vocalist of the Year Awards (four). Once I was invited to her home on Old Hickory Lake near Lebanon, Tennessee and joined her and her husband Narvel Blackstock on their boat and had the opportunity to observe how far she came from those early days.

Blackstock has been a great business partner and helped McEntire reinvent herself over the years. I give him a lot of credit for her transformation into a television and Broadway star.

Doug Hall's Vox Jox column in *Billboard* on December 7th noted that Bob Pittman was leaving the program director slot at WNBC to become director of pay television at Warner Cable. Hall mentioned me as his possible replacement, but quoted me as saying that I was very happy at WHN.

Barbara Mandrell sat in as a guest deejay during Del De Montreux's morning show in December.

Dan Abernathy recalls: "WCBS weatherman Bob Harris called himself 'Doctor' as if he had a PhD and demanded that everyone call him 'Doctor Bob' because 'I worked hard for that.' Then an anonymous letter prompted WCBS to investigate his credentials. WCBS found that he had left college without a degree and he was fired, but no one questioned his competence. Over a decade, Harris had worked for WCBS-TV and WOR radio, before joining all-news WCBS. I saw Nick Verbitsky in the hallway and said, 'Nick, I've got a great idea, a great promotion for you to show what a good guy you are. You hire Dr. Bob and then take out a full page ad in the *New York Times* with his picture, your picture and say that you've hired him for WHN and that every good man deserves a second chance.' Nick looked at me and said, 'You just stick to that news stuff that you do and leave the heavy thinking to others.' I giggled and went about my duties in the newsroom. Later in the day I met up with Ed Salamon. I gave the same pitch (just kidding around) to him. He looked at me and said 'So this is where Verbitsky got that idea that he's been bugging me about all morning.' Two weeks later, Harris was hired by WNEW. WNEW Vice President Mel Karmazin was quoted as saying 'We think Bob Harris is the best weatherman in New York, regardless of whether he ever got a degree.'"

Dan Abernathy's efforts to make WHN's news interesting

may have sometimes gone over the line. It was great radio that was compelling for listeners and much different from the staid coverage of WCBS and WINS, so I would always defend him. As a result of Abernathy's aggressiveness, WHN would frequently scoop those all news stations on major stories. As a bonus, WHN's microphone flag with our logo was always front and center at news conferences, which meant exposure on local television each evening. However, Abernathy allegedly attempted to stir up a group of Muslim protesters by calling them "rag heads" in an effort to get a good sound bite from their reaction. It was a term he had used on the air.

Although I recall Abernathy's termination at WHN to be related to that incident, he has a different recollection. Neil Rockoff had remained with Storer as their stations were being sold, but once Mutual bought WHN, Rockoff was no longer associated with the station. Abernathy recalls that he and Nick Verbitsky had frequent arguments about how WHN advertisers were treated whenever they were in the news and that Rockoff would mediate the disputes in Abernathy's favor. Once Rockoff was gone Abernathy says, "I lasted probably another two weeks before Nick bounced me onto the hard New York streets."

In December, Dirk Van became WHN's news director. He had been a general assignment reporter for WCBS radio. Dirk returned WHN to a more conventional news presentation. He had great relationships with the public officials and was able to get the mayor and governor to the station and to station events.

That same month *Electric Horseman*, an adventure and romance feature film starring Robert Redford, Jane Fonda and Willie Nelson and directed by Sydney Pollack was released. The film had a country music soundtrack, which provided WHN with hits by Nelson including "My Heroes Have Always Been Cowboys," "Midnight Rider," and "Mamas Don't Let Your Babies Grow Up to Be Cowboys," which helped draw moviegoers to country radio.

Alan Colmes was asked to do stand-up comedy at WHN's annual Christmas party for staff and key advertisers each year. This included his jokes about staff members. Colmes remembers "WHN threw the most fabulous Christmas parties for the staff and for clients high atop the New York Hilton, and I would be asked to do some stand-up at these events, but kept my job in spite of it. I also learned that Perdue chicken magnate Frank Perdue was an accomplished dancer."

The December 14th issue of *The Gavin Report* featured an article about the effect that the crossover from pop to country was having on country record production. Gavin quoted me; "As artists demonstrated that country success could be compatible with MOR and pop success, record companies began to employ more sophisticated production techniques in recording country artists to make them competitive with pop artists who were becoming successful in the country market."

Dan Taylor began the WHN overnight shift on December 21st. At the age of 21, Taylor became the youngest air personality on the AM dial in New York. According to an article in the Bridgeport Post, just four years earlier he was doing PA announcements at New Canaan High School in Bridgeport, Connecticut. I called him "the boy wonder."

"She Believes In Me" by Kenny Rogers was the No. 1 hit of the year on WHN. It was really Kenny's year on WHN. He placed four songs in the year end top twenty, and others in the Top 105 both alone and as duets with Dottie West.

CHAPTER EIGHT
1980

"Stand by Me" – Mickey Gilley (1980)

WHN's 1980 ad campaign featured subway posters with simply an artist's name and image and "WHN 1050." Every time WHN would begin a new ad campaign, the station would be deluged with requests from listeners seemingly willing to pay any price for one of the three by five foot subway posters. However, the posters were never made available to the public, until this year. WHN ran extra copies of the Elvis poster, which featured multiple images of Presley, and they became one the station's most popular contest prizes. On January 8th, WHN celebrated the anniversary of Presley's birth with a three hour broadcast of Elvis' concert recordings. In a press release, Nick Verbitsky noted "Each year Elvis Presley's popularity with the WHN audience continues to grow."

On January 22nd, Mickey Gilley did a live concert broadcast from the Lone Star Café, in which he previewed the songs he would play in the film *Urban Cowboy*. We requested that he not play "Cotton Eyed Joe," based on our experience with the audience participation during his last broadcast. WHN arranged to welcome him on the Spectacolor sign in Times Square. Other live broadcasts from the Lone Star Café that month included Jacky Ward, Doug Sahm, the Bellamy Brothers and Johnny Paycheck.

Ed Salamon

Coal Miner's Daughter was another country music themed hit movie that year. Sissy Spacek, who played Loretta Lynn, had a big WHN hit with her version of Lynn's "Coal Miner's Daughter" as a result, but the movie had a bigger effect in calling attention to Loretta Lynn's own music, especially her older songs. Spacek and Lynn both were guest deejays during Mike Fitzgerald's show on February 7th to promote the film. Fitzgerald recalls asking Lynn if she could tell who was singing as Spacek's version of the song was playing. Lynn could not tell her own version of the song from Sissy's. The story is that Lynn approved Spacek to play her in the film from a photo, not knowing whether or not she could sing.

New York Governor Hugh Carey sat in as a WHN guest deejay on February 8th. After stumbling over an introduction to a song, Carey quipped "I'll never get a job at THIS station." Live broadcasts from the Lone Star Café that month included Big Al Downing, John Wesley Ryles and Razzy Bailey.

That same month, *Billboard* announced its 1979 radio awards. WHN's Mike Fitzgerald won as Major Market Country Air Personality only two years after coming to the format.

On March 20th, WHN held a 5th anniversary party at the elegant Tavern on the Green for clients and staff. Artists including Mickey Gilley, Robert Gordon and Chip Taylor also attended. Ray Benson was frequently in New York around that time hanging with fellow Texans Doug Sahm and Kinky Friedman. Ray offered Asleep At The Wheel to play at the party. When Asleep At The Wheel set their amplifiers and equipment up in the Crystal Room, the restaurant's management insisted that the performance be cancelled. They were afraid that the sound would blow the windows out. I had to explain this to Ray and invite him and the band to attend as guests. Ray was understanding and the gentleman I've always known him to be. Asleep At The Wheel had their first national top ten country hit in 1975 with "The Letter That Johnny Walker Read," but beyond that their album cuts were a staple of Jessie's show, as they had been on the evening show at WEEP. In fact, group leader Ray Benson credited that early airplay with the group's ability to work in the Pittsburgh area early in the group's career.

Variety, the show business bible for live entertainment, would review some of the live concerts WHN broadcast from the Lone Star Café. *Variety's* Wednesday, April 23, 1980 edition reviewed the Jim Ed Brown and Helen Cornelius show, calling the Lone Star Café a "Greenwich Village, N.Y. honkytonk." It noted their 1978 version of "You Don't Bring Me Flowers," which was a big WHN hit, as a high point.

Jessie recalls, "As a publicity stunt, I was engaged in a trade of sorts. Tennis ace Vitas Gerulaitis was going to come to be a guest DJ at WHN and I was going to get to play a set of tennis with Billie Jean King at Madison Square Garden. Me in short white pants in front of 40,000 people, yikes! In order for me not to make a complete fool of myself, I trained for a couple of months with the coach of the New York Apples, the World Team Tennis franchise. I worked at this endeavor hard. In fact, so hard that I wound up with frequently blistered fingers. So I had taken to traveling with a first aid kit bandages, gauze, adhesive, and of course, my obligatory Swiss Army knife. This was back before the TSA was confiscating these things.

"One night, Waylon Jennings came to town, and I got invited to his suite at the illustrious Plaza Hotel for a night of revelry. Food, which wasn't actually being consumed, was being delivered by room service pretty much on the hour, along with ice and more booze of every description. Everyone was in 'high' spirits, shall we say, when Waylon pulled out a Jessi Colter cassette of brand new music that he wanted to share with me. The only problem was the tape had snapped. I said not to worry, and pulled out my Band Aids, and proceeded to spend the next forty five minutes splicing the tape with one of the handy blades and scissors. And Hallelujah, I got it to work, though it was for one time only, before the extra adhesive oozed out and made the whole thing a gooey mess. But the operation was successful, if only for one play. That night I got to hear some brand spanking new Jessi music. (. . . and then the party ensued until the morning light. . . .)

"I totally made a fool of myself playing Billie Jean in exhibition at Madison Square Garden shortly thereafter. I had not trained under the lights, and lost the ball in their glare upon my first service. It bounced several times, much to the delight of the audience and Billie Jean. Me, I was mortified!"

In March, Mutual Broadcasting systems bought WHN from Storer for $14 million in cash, more than four million dollars greater than Storer's 1962 purchase price and a record, at the time for the sale of a New York radio station and the second highest price paid for a radio station to that time.

A substantial reason for Mutual's interest in the station was the desire for a New York City outlet for their programming. Mutual wanted to air their newscasts at the top of the hour, instead of :55 and add a second shorter network newscast on the half hour. I was able to negotiate a compromise wherein WHN would air newscasts incorporating network reports at twenty minutes after the hour and ten minutes before the hour, thus maintaining the ability to sweep both the bottom and top of the hour with music.

Live broadcasts from the Lone Star Café that month included the Earl Scruggs Review, Freddy Fender, Bill Anderson, Jeannie Pruett and Gail Davies.

MDJ records, an independent label distributed by Nationwide Sound, released "My Home's in Alabama" by Alabama. Unlike the Oak Ridge Boys, or the Statler Brothers, this was not only a vocal group, but a self contained band. WHN immediately added it, to the surprise of Nationwide's Joe and Betty "Mama Hype" Gibson, who never felt WHN played enough of the small labels they distributed. Listeners loved the record and it became a national country hit. MDJ presented me with a plaque in appreciation for helping to break the record. I was in the audience at the Country Radio Seminar that year when the group performed on the New Faces Show. The show's policy was that all acts performed with an orchestra of Nashville session musicians; they had never encountered a self-contained act. Alabama was made to perform as a vocal trio (drummer Mark Herndon had not sung on the record). Nevertheless, they impressed RCA records so much that they signed them to a major label recording contract. They would ultimately win an award from the Academy of Country Music for Group of the Decade. Pam Green and I would socialize with the group whenever they came to New York and I still see Randy Owen, Teddy Gentry, Jeff Cook and Mark individually around Nashville on a regular basis.

In April, WHN guest deejays included Jim Ed Brown and Helen Cornelius, Billie Jo Spears and Tommy and Toy Caldwell of the Marshall Tucker Band. Tommy Caldwell died in an automobile accident nine days after his WHN appearance.

Live broadcasts from the Lone Star Café that month include Jim Ed Brown and Helen Cornelius and Billie Jo Spears.

WHN began playing "Tired of Toein' The Line" by Rocky Burnette. The song "Rock Billy Boogie" and by association, the term "rockabilly" is said to be named after Rocky and his cousin Billy Burnette (Dorsey's son). No other country stations followed on this one, but it became a top ten pop hit.

Vince Gill had what was probably his first airplay on country radio in May when WHN began playing "Let Me Love You Tonight" by Pure Prairie League on which he sang lead. The song did not make the national country charts and Gill's solo records wouldn't be promoted to country radio for another four years.

Bronco Billy, a country themed movie starring Clint Eastwood, was premiered in New Orleans. Pam Green and I were invited to attend. We both spent time with Eastwood and Green got to interview him. WHN played three songs from the movie: Eastwood's duet with Merle Haggard "Bar Room Buddies," Ronnie Milsap's "Cowboys And Clowns" and Merle Haggard's "Misery And Gin."

WHN guest deejays for May included Stephanie Winslow, Charlie Daniels, Emmylou Harris, the Gatlins and Bobby Bare. Live broadcasts from the Lone star Café include Stephanie Winslow, Joe Sun, and Bobby Bare.

On June 1st Lee Arnold and Jessie were the emcees for the Country Sunday outdoor music festival at Giants Stadium in New Jersey. WHN broadcast much of the concert that included Johnny Cash, Waylon Jennings, Eddie Rabbitt and Asleep at the Wheel. It was attended by 30,000 listeners and called New York's largest country event.

That same month *Radio and Records* ran an interview with me in which I discussed the inclusiveness of WHN's playlist ranging from the Eagles, Dan Fogelberg, Bob Seger, and Rupert Holmes to Eddy Arnold and Merle Haggard. I explained that we often have to turn down commercials from advertisers whose spots don't fit the sound of the station. Many country versions of commercials were actually condescending to country listeners and WHN would choose to play the version intended for mainstream radio instead. That same month *Record World* ran an article "Country Radio Makes Major Market Inroads" saying, "At New York's immensely successful country station WHN, program director Ed Salamon is acutely aware that his listeners' tastes run in different directions. 'Nobody is more like us in playing things that might be considered pop by the country community,' said Salamon."

Charlie Daniels, Bobby Bare, Johnny Paycheck, Jerry Jeff Walker, Robert Gordon and the New Riders of the Purple Sage performed at a concert in Madison Square Garden to benefit Myasthenia Gravis. WHN broadcast the show live.

Roy Orbison finally made the national country charts via

a duet with Emmylou Harris "That Lovin' You Feelin' Again" from the movie *Roadie*. Though they had not charted country, Orbison's hits were all staples in the WHN library. Orbison never appeared on the station because his manager, Wesley Rose, insisted that he not be considered a country artist.

That same month the movie *Urban Cowboy* was released. It featured New Jersey native John Travolta, who had recently starred in *Saturday Night Fever*. Just as that movie about New York night life had sparked a disco fad, *Urban Cowboy*, set in Pasadena, Texas, sparked interest in country music. While I welcomed any additional listeners to WHN audience, it was obvious that that majority of those listeners would be gone chasing the next musical fad that came along. It became more challenging to identify and serve the tastes of the station's core audience. I remember seeing an advance showing of *Urban Cowboy* in a small screening room off Columbus Circle. Walking into the movie, I was concerned about how the film would portray the characters. Any media that promoted negative stereotypes of country music listeners was bad for WHN. Listeners did not want to be associated with hicks and bumpkins, nor did advertisers find them attractive prospects. I was greatly relieved to see the characters in the movie portrayed sympathetically. The movie provided WHN with a number of hits, including "Lookin' For Love" by Johnny Lee, "Stand By Me" by Mickey Gilley, "The Devil Went Down To Georgia" by Charlie Daniels, "Could I Have This Dance" by Anne Murray and "Love The World Away" by Kenny Rogers. Whether or not *Urban Cowboy* did for country music what *Saturday Night Fever* did for disco, it certainly made New York movie goers curious about WHN.

WHN live broadcasts from the Lone Star Café included Merle Haggard and Asleep at the Wheel.

Mutual had asked me to produce country radio specials for them to syndicate. I agreed, providing I could do so as outside projects for additional compensation. The first idea they accepted was a two hour program *The Johnny Cash Silver Anniversary Special*. To create a separation from the specials and my WHN/Mutual employment, I recorded the interview with Johnny Cash at Narwood Productions. Narwood had syndicated Lee Arnold's *Country Cookin'* show, and I was friends with owner Ted Levan and Ellen Silver, who ran the operation. I asked Paul Evans if I could borrow his Martin guitar, just in case I could coax Cash to illustrate the writing of some of his hits by playing part of them (which Cash did). Shelby Singleton of Sun records was kind enough to go through their archives and provide me with outtakes and studio chatter from John's earliest recordings. Everything worked perfectly and I hired WHN creative services producer Fred Siebert to do the final editing of the show. Mutual distributed it for airing on the 4th of July weekend and it was carried by 440 stations, making it the most successful program they had in a long time. The show also won a *Billboard* magazine award as Network or Syndicated Special of the Year. Since I owned the interview, I also sold it as a cover story in the July/August edition of *Country Weekly*.

In July, WHN gave away tickets for the movie *Roadie*, which starred Meat Loaf, Deborah Harry and Alice Cooper, among others, but contained a few country songs. Ray Benson, leader of the group Asleep At The Wheel, which also appeared in the movie, came to WHN and voiced the promo spots.

That same month, Nick Verbitsky was named senior vice president of operations and stations for Mutual, which owned WCFL in addition to WHN. Verbitsky promoted WHN general sales manager Brian Moors to station manager. WHN director of national sales, Dick Kelley, replaced Moors as general sales manager.

I was asked to reverse the fate of Mutual's other owned radio station, WCFL in Chicago and so became de-facto national program director for Mutual stations. In the late 60s, WCFL programmed by John Rook was one of America's leading Top

40 radio stations. Mutual bought the station in 1979 and programmed the station with shows compatible with the philosophies of Mutual's owners, who also owned the Amway Corporation. *Chicago Sun-Times* columnist Gary Deeb called WCFL the dullest news and talk format in captivity. "The result," Deeb said, was "the least-listened-to 50,000 watt AM radio station in broadcast history."

Given my involvement, there were industry rumors that the station would change to a country format to challenge WMAQ, but that was never intended. I recommended capitalizing on the station's image as "Super CFL" and switching to an oldies format. I hired Dave Martin, program director at WFYR, a Chicago oldies FM station, as WCFL's program director. Martin hired Johnny Kay as assistant program director. He later went on to famously program KOST in Los Angeles as Jhani Kaye. I suggested Chicago air personality Fred Winston for mornings. I had remembered Fred from mornings at KQV in Pittsburgh. It was rumored that legendary radio consultant Paul Drew was consulting the station, but he was not, it was me. After my involvement, the station morphed into adult contemporary music before being sold to a new owner and contemporary Christian programming.

WHN guest deejays in July included John Conlee, Tom T. Hall, Charly McClain and Rex Allen, Jr. Live broadcasts from the Lone Star Café included John Conlee and Rex Allen, Jr.

Epic records released Johnny Paycheck's *New York Town* album, which had been recorded during a WHN live broadcast at the Lone Star Café. When I received the album, I was surprised to hear the introduction by WHN's Mike Fitzgerald open the album as was Mike. The record company had neglected to get his permission, and in fact, had failed to even credit him on the album. The intro was typical for the broadcasts, where the master of ceremonies would recite a succession of the titles of the artist's biggest hits. It was a technique I had learned from James Brown, who had his announcers introduce his show that way, most famously documented on his 1963 *Live at the Apollo* album. After some discussion between the parties, Mike agreed to accept a token amount in exchange for his release to let his voice be used on the album. "In Memory Of A Memory" was the song that was released to radio, but WHN played the other side "New York Town," thinking it better for our market.

Donny and Marie Osmond sat in as guest deejays during Lee Arnold's midday show. For the past several years, they had starred in the ABC network prime time series *Donny and Marie*. On their show, Marie would sing "I'm a little bit country," and Donny would respond, "I'm a little bit rock and roll." Marie had a major country hit with "Paper Roses" and would resume her country hit making career a few years later. Other WHN guest deejays that month included Freddie Hart, Margo Smith and Bobby Bare.

In August, WHN broadcast a series of concerts from Belmont Park in Long Island. They included Bobby Bare with the Bellamy Brothers and Donna Fargo, Johnny Paycheck and Mickey Gilley with Johnny Lee.

Mutual hired Lee Arnold to host its annual "Jamboree In The Hills" live country concert which the network broadcast on Labor Day weekend. On September 8th at noon, WHN finally got FM competition. Jazz formatted WRVR switched formats to country and call letters to WKHK. The station, known as "one-o-six kicks" on the air, kicked off with with Waylon Jennings' "Are You Ready For The Country." The owners, Viacom, owned the successful KIKK in Houston. The new station air staff included an old friend from 13-Q in Pittsburgh, Batt Johnson, who made the transition from jazz to country, making him the second black country deejay in New York after J.J. Ramey. He had worked at WRVR, and would at WKHK all the time it was a country station. Viacom national program director and former KIKK program director Bill Figenshu and former KIKK general manager Al Greenfield came to WKHK in the same positions.

WHN: When New York City Went Country

Most pundits said WKHK would quickly put WHN out of business, as was the norm with most FM music stations that attacked AM stations with the same format. But that was not to be.

WRVR listeners protested the format switch. A reported 200 protesters picketed Viacom offices chanting "The airwaves belong to the people." Some carried placards calling the format switch "Jazz genocide."

WKHK mounted what the *New York Times* reported to be a $1 million ad campaign, "New York Is Putting Its Boots On," with the Statue of Liberty wearing cowboy boots. WKHK hired former WHN morning personality Larry Kenney for that same day part and ran a television campaign that featured him.

WHN guest deejays in September included Donna Fargo, Charlie Daniels, Dave Rowland and Sugar and Dottie West. Live concert broadcasts from the Lone Star Café included Freddy Fender and Dobie Gray.

Forbes magazine's October 13th issue carried a picture of Nick Verbitsky in front of a WHN subway poster with the quote "Whatever the reasons—the fastest growing segment of popular music today is called 'country'." *Forbes* noted that following WHN's success, stations were switching to country: "Nearly 400 have switched in the last two years alone." In the same article, Ben Karol of New York's King Karol record stores said, "Country music is the trend of the 80s."

The TV series *Barabara Mandrell and the Mandrell Sisters* premiered on NBC this year. In addition to hosts Barbara, Louise and Irlene Mandrell, the show featured mostly country musical guests and comedy sketches. WHN air personalities talked a lot about this show, as it was another medium that interested New Yorkers in country music.

Live concert broadcasts from the Lone Star Café in October included Charly McClain and Jeannie Pruett.

John Hartford had agreed to perform live on Jessie's show in November while he was in town to appear at The Bottom Line.

Ed Salamon

Although he hadn't had hit country singles, Hartford was well known to the WHN audience from appearances on *The Smothers Brothers Comedy Hour*, *The Glen Campbell Goodtime Hour* and *The Johnny Cash Show*. Jessie played a number of tracks from his album. A few hours before his performance, his manager called and said that Hartford required a sheet of plywood of a specific dimension as a condition for his appearance. It wasn't easy to quickly locate the plywood in midtown Manhattan, but Pam Green was able to do so. Hartford clog danced on the plywood while he sang and performed. That evening WHN presented country dancing on New York radio.

In November, Anne Murray sold out a performance at Radio City Music Hall. After the show I presented her with WHN Listeners' Choice Awards as a favorite Female Vocalist of the Year for 1979 and 1980. A photo of me presenting Murray with the awards was carried in the December 6th edition of *Billboard*.

WHN guest deejays in November include Levon Helm of the Band and Gene Watson.

When John Lennon died on the evening of December 8th, Jessie was on the air. I was listening to the station at the time and I remember her breaking in with the announcement. That was the right thing to do because, although we did not play John Lennon's music, he was a prominent New Yorker well known to our listeners. After she reported Lennon's death, she followed with Alabama's recent somber hit "Why Lady Why."

The December 13th issue of *Billboard* reported the program I produced for Mutual, "Country Music Countdown 1980" was expected to set a modern record for clearance of a network radio special when it aired on 616 stations, including in 142 of the nation's top 150 markets. Anne Murray and Mike Fitzgerald were the hosts of the show, which included interviews with many of the artists that hits that year. I was embarrassed by the trade ad that Mutual used to celebrate the show's success because it had a "sold out" banner sniped across Anne Murray's head.

WHN: WHEN NEW YORK CITY WENT COUNTRY

"Lookin' For Love" by Johnny Lee from the movie *Urban Cowboy* was WHN's No. 1 hit of the year. Others in the top five, in order, were "Don't Fall In Love With A Dreamer" by Kenny Rogers and Kim Carnes, "It's Like We Never Said Goodbye" by Crystal Gayle, "Love The World Away" by Kenny Rogers and "On The Road Again" by Willie Nelson.

CHAPTER NINE
1981

"I Was Country When Country Wasn't Cool" – Barbara Mandrell (1981)

Alabama's Jeff Cook recalls, "WHN was THE station to listen to. It was in the Big Apple. It was also a pioneer in playing the music that was being pumped out at the time. They played music by Alabama!"

The Iranian hostage crisis was the name given to the fifty-two Americans who were held hostage for four hundred forty four days from November 4, 1979 to January 20, 1981, after a group of Islamists took over the American Embassy in Tehran in support of the Iranian Revolution. We learned from former hostage Mike Howland that the hostages had a tape of WHN smuggled in by a Swiss diplomat that they kept playing over and over as a valued link with home. Of course, Charlie Daniels' patriotic anthem "In America" would have been a frequently played song on that tape. Former hostages Howland and Alan Golacinski met with members of the WHN air staff, who toasted their release at the Lone Star Café.

The January 17th issue of *Billboard* carried a photo of Dolly Parton taping some promos with me for a contest we were running in connection with her movie *9 to 5*, in which three working women live out their fantasy of getting even with their boss.

Ed Salamon

I had taped the promos at a premiere Pam Green and I attended in Nashville in December. At the time, Parton's song "9 to 5" was topping the WHN charts and crossing over to Top 40 radio. The single ultimately became a million seller.

Despite WHN's role to cross records over from country to pop airplay, we heard that the Nashville offices of the record labels were now petitioning the trade magazines to have WHN removed as a reporting station to the country charts. While we defined country music simply as records that our listeners wanted to hear on WHN, the Nashville record labels defined country as the music that was marketed out of Nashville. I learned that the Nashville divisions of the labels did not get credit for the sales of records that were assigned to the label's pop divisions. Therefore, when WHN played a record that a label had assigned to its pop division, it was of no benefit to the Nashville office of that label. The revenues from the sale of those records were all credited to the pop division. Even worse, it took up a space on the charts that could have been held by a Nashville record. Trade magazines told me they felt that they were in the business of reflecting, rather than manipulating, airplay, so they refused to drop WHN as a reporting station to all of the country charts.

In February, Dan Taylor was chosen as a winner of radio syndicator Drake Chenault's Top Five Talent Search, a nationwide award recognizing America's top air personalities.

Another sign that country music was getting hipper was the release of *Your Cheating Heart*, a biography of Hank Williams by Chet Flippo, who had been senior editor of *Rolling Stone*. In addition to covering John Lennon, The Rolling Stones, Bob Dylan and the like for that magazine, he also wrote about country artists including Dolly Parton, Willie Nelson and Waylon Jennings. At the launch party for the book at the Lone Star Café snacks were served from bowls made from molded vinyl records. Flippo was a WHN listener when he served as *Rolling Stone's* New York Bureau Chief in the late 70s.

WHN: WHEN NEW YORK CITY WENT COUNTRY

Don McLean, from nearby New Rochelle, New York and best known for his 1972 hit "American Pie," released a country sounding remake of Roy Orbison's "Crying," which was in WHN's oldies rotation. Listeners loved the new version and the record became McLean's first national country hit, as well as a pop hit. He next release was a remake of the Skyliners' 1959 hit "Since I Don't Have You," which likewise was played by both pop and country radio stations. Ronnie Milsap would again successfully revive that song for country listeners in 1991.

B. J. Thomas had stopped recording secular music after his 1977 hit "Don't Worry Baby" to concentrate on gospel music. He appeared as a guest deejay to premiere "Some Love Songs Never Die," his first non-gospel record in four years.

The Burrito Brothers, successors to longtime favorites of Jessie's listeners The Flying Burrito Brothers, had signed with a Nashville label and were releasing singles to country radio. WHN played "Does She Wish She Was Single Again" and "She Belongs To Everyone But Me." They visited the station and sat in as guest deejays. Group member Skip Battin was part of the 50s duo Skip and Flip who had the hits "It Was I" and "Cherry Pie."

Rick Nelson was a guest deejay for the first time in his career when Mike Fitzgerald turned over the microphone to him. Epic promotion man Ray Free brought him to the station to promote his new Epic single "Dream Lover," a remake of Bobby Darin's 1959 hit. WHN played Nelson's older hits, including "Garden Party," "Believe What You Say," "Travelin' Man" and others in regular oldies rotation. Pam Green, who directed Nelson, recalls, "He was very quiet. I think he was probably very shy." That night Free and I went to see him perform at the Bottom Line and swapped stories with him backstage.

That same month Sylvia sat in as guest deejay as her single "Drifter" reached No. 1 on the WHN chart. The following year her record "Nobody" would cross over and become at top twenty pop hit.

Ed Salamon

Glen Campbell and Tanya Tucker were now a couple and sat in together as guest deejays in February, during Lee Arnold's shift, with Pam Green directing them. They were recording duets together, including yet another remake of Bobby Darin's 1959 hit "Dream Lover" and a new song "Why Don't We Just Sleep on it Tonight." Tanya had previously been romantically linked to Merle Haggard (twenty one years her senior), actor Don Johnson and pop star Andy Gibb. In June, I accompanied Glen to an appearance on the television show *Sesame Street* where he was promoting his appearance on the album *Sesame Country*, on which Tanya also appeared. That album won a Grammy award for its writer and producer, Dennis Scott.

I recall one evening when Campbell and Tucker were staying in New York, Campbell showed up late to a Tom Jones benefit for the Friars Club that I attended. He walked in and was seated while Jones was in the middle of his performance. Glen was being openly affectionate to the young lady who accompanied him. He was obviously aware that in front of an audience filled with press and the entertainment industry, word would get back to Tanya. Creating even more attention, he left shortly before the end of the performance. Glen and Tanya were on the cover of *People* magazine multiple times and seemingly in every tabloid that year, and they created a lot of interest every time they appeared on WHN.

In June, Glen and Tanya would return to perform a live concert broadcast for WHN from the Belmont Park Race Track. In his book, Rhinestone Cowboy, Glen details the constant arguments, including verbal and physical abuse during this time fueled by their drinking and use of cocaine. It seemed that each would do whatever they could to torment the other. Newsman Gene Ladd produced and hosted a Sunday morning interview show, In The Public Interest, which featured celebrities. He recalls, "I remember one interview that did not make it to air. Glen Campbell and Tanya Tucker started off pretty straight, but soon started a discussion that could not be aired. I left them in the studio and they were in there for a long time before their people could get them out."

As remarkable as that was, that was not Gene's most outrageous encounter with an artist at WHN; "Robert Goulet was sitting in with Bob Jones in A, the big studio in the back. I went in to give a newscast. Goulet was trying to break me up. He set my script on fire. When that did not work, he unzipped and exposed himself. I threw the burning script at his exposed parts and promptly went to the spot, because then I broke up."

Ladd also recalls highlights of his Sunday morning show *In The Public Interest* included "Brenda Lee and her husband talking about their challenges as parents of teens. Mrs. Conway Twitty discussing her family and challenges keeping Twitty City going after Conway's death. Dolly, who was in NY perhaps most frequently, talking about the strength of her marriage and plans for Dollywood to make jobs for her family and community. A tearful talk with Loretta Lynn about her son's death and her marriage. I will always cherish George and Tammy talking about how much they loved each other even when they did not, and questioning if their relationship was driven by love or music. The most fun was with the Statler Brothers in the role of Cadillac Cowboys, saying their favorite color is chrome. Johnny Paycheck confirming that he indeed had been on the 'Cocaine Train.' I remember extending my hand when I was introduced to blind country artist Terri Gibbs who had a wonderful interview about her faith and career. Ronnie Milsap was an interesting interview talking about his childhood and his struggles. Jimmy Dean would not talk about music for more than thirty seconds, but could really sell the sausage. Placido Domingo gave us a wonderful interview when he recorded with John Denver. John Denver did not like my questions about his collaboration with the duo Fat City and the song he wrote with them 'Take Me Home, Country Roads.' Waylon Jennings was not much of a talker, but it was bona fide outlaw stuff. Johnny Cash and June were difficult, mostly because they only wanted to promote their movie about the Holy Land. Kenny Rogers, I can't forget, went on and on about how his jazz background prepared him for the ballads. Mickey Gilley was a good interview, especially talking about his cousins, Jerry Lee Lewis and preacher Jimmy Swaggart. All in all, I really enjoyed these interviews and the honesty of the people who make country music."

The February 28th issue of *Billboard* carried a photo of Pam Green and me congratulating Levon Helm after a performance at the Lone Star Café. He was promoting his MCA album *American Son*, which came about the previous year when he co-starred as Loretta Lynn's father in the movie *Coal Miner's Daughter*. He had recorded "Blue Moon of Kentucky" for the film and the record label liked what they heard and commissioned an album. We met at the station that evening. Levon sat in as a guest deejay for an hour and played a lot of the country flavored songs he had recorded with The Band, including "Up On Cripple Creek" and "The Night They Drove Ol Dixie Down." During our drive to the club Levon was very nervous about my driving, and he held onto the door tightly and would jerk away from the window when he thought I was getting too close to other cars. I tried to take his mind off the traffic by asking questions about his work with Ronnie Hawkins and Bob Dylan and reminding him of his record "He Don't Love You" by Levon and the Hawks that I had played at dances in Pittsburgh.

By this time, every Oak Ridge Boys single was an automatic add to the WHN playlist. Their new record was "Elvira" and it made a greater impact than any of their previous releases, due largely to Oaks' bass singer Richard Sterban's "oom papa mow mow" refrain. The Oaks frequently appeared on WHN as guest deejays. Lead singer Duane Allen recalls one appearance: "We landed at the airport in a snow storm. The limo did not show up, so we were already running late. We got two cabs and tipped the drivers to get us through the snow storm. The two drivers must have thought that they were in a demolition derby. We slid through lights, scraped a few parked cars, but we made it to WHN just in time for the advertised show. We literally slid into the studio. We were given spots to read and I remember seeing lines like 'SONY Trinitron' and a few other names that I was not familiar with. After each of us trying to get through the news, sports, and commercials, it was time for the weather. They turned the microphone to William Lee Golden. When it was his time to talk he just paused and paused, as we all waited. Then in his south Alabama drawl, William Lee said, 'It's gonna get cold, y'all.' Church was out. We just rolled on the floor."

The Oak's Joe Bonsall recalls another occasion when Golden's guest deejay work affected other guests at the station: "Everyone was on the floor including some New York Mets who thought it was so funny they invited us to Shea stadium that night."

By June, "Elvira" was selling so many singles in the New York area that Top 40 station WABC added it. It became the first and biggest pop hit for the Oak Ridge Boys.

In March, The Rovers sat in as guest deejays during Lee Arnold's midday show. Formerly known as The Irish Rovers, their 1968 pop hit "The Unicorn" was played by stations in many formats every St. Patrick's Day. At this time their single "Wasn't That A Party" was on both the pop and country charts.

The April issue of *Madison Avenue* carried the ad "America's leading country music station is right here in New York. WHN." This was the first ad that based WHN's No. 1 position in the country format based on cume (number of different listeners), rather than average quarter hour audience (how many people are listening at one time). While WHN had perennially had the most listeners per quarter hour, making it the most-listened-to country radio station, the country station with the most different listeners had often been Chicago's WMAQ. WMAQ's

Ed Salamon

Class A clear channel signal had a substantially greater coverage area than WHN's directional signal. At this point, WHN had surpassed WMAQ is both in listening and numbers of different listeners.

That same month, Michael Martin Murphey did a live concert broadcast from WHN from the Lone Star Café.

In June, Mike Fitzgerald emceed a live broadcast of a Johnny Cash show from Belmont Park on Long Island.

George Strait played guest deejay on Mike Fitzgerald's show when his first record "Unwound" came out. Fitzgerald says, "He was such a gentle, shy man and he still is. I cherished that time with him as I got to see his career reach unbelievable heights."

At the end of July, Jessie's contract was up and she left WHN to pursue other interests. Her replacement was Dana Lauren from KBZT-FM (K-Best), the oldies station I consulted in San Diego.

Lois Gilbert from our country competitor WKHK-FM was hired for weekends and fill-ins.

Lee Arnold's contract was up for renewal. His agent was Sandy Linzer, the successful songwriter who co-wrote "A Lover's Concerto," "Let's Hang On!," "Working My Way Back to You" and "Native New Yorker" among many others. Arnold couldn't come to terms with the station, and his contract was not renewed. Mike Fitzgerald moved from afternoon drive to Lee's midday slot. Dan Taylor moved from overnights to fill Fitzgerald's slot. Brian Kelly, who was doing overnights at WCBS-FM, was hired in the same capacity at WHN. Del De Montreux's show in morning drive was the only daypart that was not affected.

Kelly was the third consecutive overnight air personality that WHN hired from WCBS-FM. WCBS-FM was considered a very desirable station to work at. As a result, they received more talent resumes and air checks then WHN did. Their program director Joe McCoy, and Bob Vanderheyden before him, were astute judges of talent. Whereas most of the air checks WHN received were from country deejays and most of them still had a dated, middle of the road sound. At the time, AFTRA union pay scale was higher for AM than FM stations, a situation remaining from when FM was an emerging technology. So, WHN had to pay more than WCBS-FM's minimum union scale. WHN had the opportunity to listen to prospective employees live on the air and they didn't have to move from another market. I even hired the fourth overnight WCBS-FM air talent in a row later this year when I hired Chris Charles at the United Stations.

Mort Cooperman had been asking me to allow Kinky Friedman, who was a regular performer at Cooperman's Lone Star Café, to do a live concert broadcast on WHN. I wanted to be helpful to Cooperman, since he had delivered so many stars of country music for WHN live broadcasts, but I had seen Kinky's act and it consisted of sexually suggestive songs like "Homo Erectus" and references to Judaism like "They Don't Make Jews like Jesus Any More," which I felt some WHN listeners could find offensive. Mort delivered a tape of a performance Kinky had recorded with an hour of songs from his Epic and Vanguard albums that were acceptable. Many were tracks that were regularly played on Jessie's show. Cooperman said that this was the set Kinky would perform on a live broadcast. We scheduled the broadcast for midnight. That night, instead of the set promised, Friedman reverted to his normal material. We ended the broadcast during the second song. The next morning when I arrived for work there were several representatives of the Jewish Anti-Defamation League in the lobby threatening to complain to the FCC about anti-Jewish remarks made during the broadcast. Kinky Friedman was Jewish, as was Jessie, the emcee, and Ron Schiller, the technical producer. Mort Cooperman was Jewish. None of them had been offended. I, the only gentile in the mix, had been the only one concerned enough to stop the broadcast. Somehow we pacified the group, and Cooperman never again pursued the subject of a live broadcast with Friedman.

That was not my only run in with Kinky Friedman. At a WHN live broadcast with another act, Susan Storms complained that Friedman had made a rude and obscene remark to her. Perhaps influenced by my consumption of the Lone Star's famed Texas Tornados beverage, I felt compelled leave my seat to find him and correct his behavior. I don't recall whether or not I was successful in finding Friedman to confront him that evening, but Storms recalls that I "put him in his place."

Storms could be a lightning rod for unwelcome attention from male artists. One evening some of us from the station were having dinner with a star who had just charted four consecutive No. 1 songs. Storms arrived late and asked where she should sit. The artist quipped "Honey, as long as I have a face, you'll always have a place to sit." The record rep accompanying him seemed embarrassed. On another occasion, Storms recalls an up and coming star, who would later have an iconic patriotic hit, "sticking his tongue down my throat one night on his bus at the Lone Star."

MTV began on August 1st. Its programming chief was my old friend Bob Pittman. MTV's launch involved some key former WHN staffers as well. Dale Pon had left WNBC to join legendary adman George Lois in a new ad agency, LPG/Pon. That company created the campaign slogan "I want my MTV." MTV's Fred Siebert, who had replaced Pon at WHN, along with Alan Goodman, created a visual logo utilizing public domain footage of the Apollo 11 moon landing, much as Dale and Fred had created trade ads at WHN using still shots from NASA. MTV also hired WHN's audience research director, Pearl Lieberman, as a reporter and research supervisor.

WCBS-TV's evening newscast covered Mel Tillis' appearance as a WHN guest deejay.

In August, Nick Verbitsky, Frank Murphy and I resigned from Mutual to form the United Stations with Dick Clark. Clark had been hosting *Dick Clark's National Music Survey*, a current countdown show for Mutual. Murphy was vice president of Mutual's affiliate relations, the department which sold radio stations the shows and network services. Verbitsky was senior vice president of stations and operations. We all believed that the appetite for entertainment programming would grow significantly. Mutual's president, Marty Rubenstein, had met with us and told us that the network's future was in traditional news and sports programming. We saw the opportunity and formed the United Stations in September 1981. United Stations agreed to Mutual's request that I produce the year end countdown "Country Music Countdown 1981," which was hosted by the Oak Ridge Boys and Mike Fitzgerald.

Station manager Brian Moors was named to succeed Verbitsky as WHN's vice president/general manager. Moors had joined WHN in 1975 as a sales person. *Radio and Records* quoted him saying, "I have to replace Ed Salamon who's been here 6 ½ years and that's not an easy task."

Pam Green was chosen to serve as interim program director, a position she would fill between WHN program directors in the future.

Even though I continued to produce Mutual specials, Dan Taylor remembers that an agreement with Mutual prohibited any interaction between theWHN staff and those of us at the United Stations. Taylor recalls, "Naturally, I went to see Ed anyway. While we were in his office, Ed heard Dick Clark coming down the hallway and said 'Dan, quick put this bag on your head.' I obliged as Dick walked into the office. I could see through my makeshift eyes that Dick was puzzled. 'And who is this, Ed?' he asked. 'Just somebody I worked with once.' Ed then removed the bag and I spoke my name. Dick said 'You're not supposed to be here, don't you know you'll get us all in trouble?' Nevertheless, we all had a good laugh and I guess I may be the only person to have been introduced to the legendary Dick Clark with a bag over my head."

In September, WABC's top twenty included four country hits: "Queen of Hearts" by Juice Newton, "I Don't Need You"

Ed Salamon

and "Share Your Love With Me," both by Kenny Rogers and "There's No Getting Over You" by Ronnie Milsap.

New York mayor Ed Koch proclaimed October as Country Music Month at a ceremony at City Hall attended by CMA Chairman of the Board and CBS Record president Bruce Lundvall, Chairman of Country Music Month Committee and Peer Southern publishing's Roy Horton, and WHN's Brian Moors, Pam Green and Dana Lauren.

George Strait made a few guest deejay appearances and did at least one live concert broadcast from the Lone Star Café. Pam Green recalls, "He was a guest deejay on October 8th, at the time his first hit 'Unwound' was on the chart. There was a picture taken of me, George, his manager, Erv Woolsey and Mike Fitzgerald in the studio that was included in the booklet for George's first box set, *Strait Out Of The Box,* when it was released in September 1995."

"Hats Off To Country," a concert featuring Larry Gatlin and Janie Fricke, played Madison Square Garden on October 24th. Terri Gibbs, who won the CMA Horizon Award that year, was also on the bill. Dan Taylor and Dana Lauren were there with Pam Green. Lee Arnold recalls interviewing Gatlin backstage at Madison Square Garden: "Doing an interview with Larry and the boys during that period was a challenge. It was like playing Russian roulette. You did not know what shape they would be in, and most times it was a string of expletives, and they could not keep their minds on the questions or answers. One time at Madison Square Garden, I did an interview with Larry that lasted forty five minutes. I barely got one 'voice bite' out of it, merely thirty seconds worth was all I could use. The rest of the tape was unusable." Pam Green recalls, "Larry was a little crazy that day, but I didn't realize until he checked himself into rehab in the mid 80s that he had a problem with drugs and alcohol. He covered it very well. I rarely even saw him drink a beer."

WHN's new program director was Dene Hallam from

WWWW, Detroit, where Howard Stern had worked until it changed format to country. I first met Hallam in 1976 through Pete Kanze. Hallam was doing part time air work on a Top 40 station in Philadelphia and told me that he would do anything to work full time in radio. I was impressed by his audition tape and his intelligence. I had an offer to consult a radio station in Harrisburg. The owner, Herb Scott, was willing to pay only a very small amount for staff. I thought I could teach Hallam how to do the format and he could be both program director and morning man for a paltry $185 a week. Hallam and Scott agreed, and Hallam switched WFEC from Top 40 to country in 1977. I asked Hallam to hire Alan Furst, who had been an intern for me when I programmed WEEP and later again at WHN. The station air staff also included Barry Mardit, who would follow Dene as program director of WFEC and later WWWW, Detroit. Although the results were phenomenal, after less than a year, Scott asked that I replace Hallam as they weren't getting along. By then I was consulting WEEP, so I moved Hallam there as co-program director with Robbie Roman, so as not to demote either of them. That didn't work out, so I moved Robbie to K-Best (KBZT), a start up oldies station I was consulting in San Diego. The general manager wasn't happy with Roman, so I moved Hallam there and Roman came back to WHN. After about a year at KBZT, Hallam left to program WWWW in Detroit. When Roman wasn't promoted to WHN program director, he resigned from the station and moved back to Pittsburgh.

At WWWW, Hallam had been playing "Perhaps Love" a duet by John Denver and Placido Domingo. He immediately added it at WHN. Although the song never made the national country charts, WHN received press coverage when Hallam invited Domingo to sit in as a guest deejay on WHN. At a time when most major market country radio programmers had the philosophy "we don't make the hits, we just play them," Hallam continued WHN's role in developing artists and songs for the format.

Ed Salamon

WHN's No. 1 song of 1981 was Dolly Parton's "9 to 5." Even though he had died in 1977, Elvis Presley placed two newly released songs among the Top 105 WHN songs of that year, "Lovin' Arms" and "Guitar Man." Although they didn't make the national country charts, Dan Fogelberg's "Same Old Lang Syne" and "Hard To Say" also were among WHN's top songs of the year.

When the Mutual Broadcasting Company bought WHN in 1980, Ed Salamon began producing country radio specials for the network. Here Dolly Parton takes over by grabbing the Mutual mike and sitting on Salamon's lap.

At the height of *The Urban Cowboy's* popularity, artists whose music appeared in the film were frequent guests on WHN. Here Johnny Lee, whose "Lookin' For Love" from the movie topped the national country charts for weeks, is surrounded by Pam Green and Robbie Roman, Brian Moore and Lee Arnold.

This 1980 sales promotion piece referred to WHN as a personality rather than a country music station. The WHN airs staff included five fulltime and three part time deejays.

New York Mayor Ed Koch (second from left) accepts WHN's "Man of the Year" award from Mutual Broadcasting Company president Marty Rubenstein, Ed Salamon, Mutual senior vice president/WHN general manager Nick Verbitsky and WHN news director Dirk Van.(Photo by Lifetime Pictures)

Shel Silverstein may best be remembered for his children's books, or as a *Playboy* cartoonist, but he was also a successful country songwriter. Many of his songs were recorded by Bobby Bare. Backstage after a 1980 broadcast are Dan Taylor, CBS Records president Bruce Lundvall, Lone Star Café's Bill Dick, Silverstein, Bare, Ed Salamon and Columbia Records VP Ed Hynes.

John Schneider, who played Bo Duke on the CBS television series *The Dukes of Hazzard*, was a WHN listener from Mount Kisco, New York. When in the city, he would stop by the station to say hello. In this 1980 photo, he spontaneously showed up at the station in his jogging suit and said hello to Nick Verbitsky and Ed Salamon. WHN's airplay helped to make his version of "It's Now Or Never" a country and pop crossover hit the following year.

During the Iran Hostage Crisis, the fifty two Americans that were held hostage for 444 days listened to smuggled tapes of WHN. Welcoming hostages home in February 1981 are WHN station manager Brian Moors, former hostage Alan Golacinski, newsman Bernard Gershon, former hostage Michael Howland, Ed Salamon and Dirk Van.

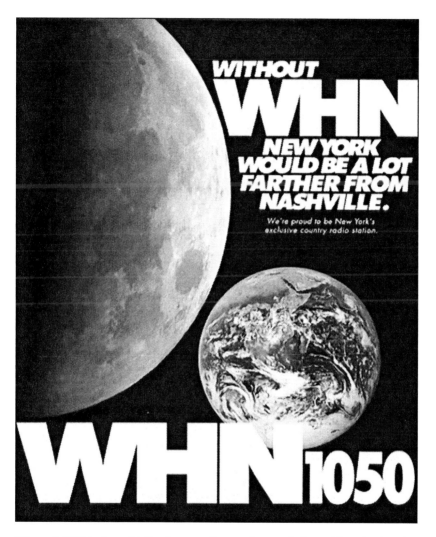

Although WHN often didn't reference its country music format in ads aimed at potential New York listeners, the station took pride in representing its country affiliation in industry ads. This ad was designed by WHN creative services director Fred Siebert utilizing NASA photographs as Siebert would later do to promote MTV in its famous "man on the moon" logo.

Mike Fitzgerald directs Rick Nelson during Nelson's first appearance as a guest deejay on radio.

Johnny Cash performed on a live WHN broadcast from Belmont Park in Long Island in 1981, where he was introduced by afternoon personality Mike Fitzgerald.

George Jones shares a joke with Ed Salamon during a photo opportunity with The Oak Ridge Boys, visiting WHN in March 1981 to promote their then current single "Elvira". Standing left to right are Salamon, Brian Moors, Jones, Oak Joe Bonsall, Lee Arnold Seated are Oaks Duane Allen and Richard Sterban. A photo from this session was used in the booklet for Jones' 1982 Time Life album set.

Glen Campbell and Tanya Tucker frequently visited WHN together in the early 80s. In this 1981 shot Campbell encourages Tucker to smile for the camera as Brian Moors and Ed Salamon look on.

The Gatlins receive their WHN Listeners' Choice Award as Group of the Year from Brian Moors and Lee Armold. Shown left to right, Steve Gatlin, Larry Gatlin, Rudy Gatlin, Moors and Arnold.

WHN played Placido Domingo's duet with John Denver, "Perhaps Love" and Domingo sat in as a guest deejay. Despite Denver's hot streak on country radio, his "Some Days Are Diamonds (Some Days Are Stone)" had just been a top ten hit, his duet with Domingo did not make the national country charts.

CHAPTER TEN
1982

"A Country Boy Can Survive" – Hank Williams, Jr. (1982)

After an eight month absence, Lee Arnold was rehired by Dene Hallam. Air shifts were shortened to accommodate six full time air personalities rather than five. Arnold also began doing network programming for Mutual. Arnold was featured on the cover of the *Cash Box 1982 Country Radio Directory*, which was published on February 27th to coincide with the Country Radio Seminar in Nashville.

Pam Green recalls that when a country artist appeared at any large venue around New York, Hallam would program an hour of their music beginning as the concert was letting out. He also had flyers promoting WHN put on the windshields of every car in the parking lots of the arena.

In March, *Billboard* presented its 1980 and 1981 country radio awards at a dinner during the 13th annual Country Radio Seminar in Nashville. WHN won as 1980 Country Station of the Year and new general manager Brian Moors accepted that award. I accepted awards as Program Director of the Year for both 1980 and 1981 for my work at WHN as well as the award for Network or Syndicated Special of the Year for *The Johnny Cash Silver Anniversary Special*.

Roger Miller was guest deejay on April 12th. Best remembered for his country and pop hits of the 60s, "King of The Road," "Dang Me" and "Chug-A-Lug," he had not had a hit in almost a decade. He was soon to remedy that a couple months after this appearance with "Old Friends," a duet with Willie Nelson (with Ray Price).

Dana Lauren resigned from WHN to join Country Music Radio Network that United Stations intended to begin to provide live country programming twenty four hours a day, seven days a week. Unfortunately, that project was cancelled and Lauren returned to California.

Shelia York, from KILT in Houston, replaced Lauren in the evening time slot. She has a great story, and since she is now a professional novelist (the Lauren Atwill Mystery series), I'll have her tell it in her own words: "In May 1982, I was out of radio and living in Houston on a small income from radio and TV commercials. The station I'd worked for, KILT-AM, had changed its programming several months before, from light rock to country, and the new program director didn't think I was a country music sort of girl. I still have no idea what that meant. I did notice, though, that when he fielded his new line-up, there were no country music girls at all.

"In the last week in May, I got a phone call out of the blue from Dene Hallam. He was looking for a woman to do the evening shift. One of his friends had heard me on the air at some point, and recorded part of my show. He played it for Dene over the phone, and Dene tracked me down. Over Memorial Day weekend, I flew to New York to talk to him and GM Brian Moors. They offered me the job and wanted me to start within a week. I flew to Houston, told my husband, 'Sell the house, sell the car.' I packed a bag and flew back. David was left to do everything.

"I had grown up in Tennessee, and my mother was a country music fan. She never made much out of it, and I have since wondered if she was a little embarrassed, as it was part of her roots in West Virginia and east Kentucky coal mining towns. People had very uninformed opinions about folks who grew up in the hills back then (and probably still do). But mom always turned on the Saturday afternoon country music shows on Nashville TV, like *Flatt & Scruggs* and *The Porter Wagoner Show* (with Dolly Parton), and we'd watch together. She taught me country music (and baseball). Then I lived in Texas during what was called the 'Urban Cowboy' days, and the enormous popularity of 'Waylon, Willie and the boys'.

"Nevertheless, I now found myself on the air at the biggest country music station in the world, in a city that could easily overwhelm. Del De Montreux, Mike Fitzgerald, Lee Arnold, Dan Taylor, Brian Kelly, Pam Green (our music director), Gene Ladd (news) and Eda Galeno (Dene's assistant) all welcomed me warmly, and the ones who worked in the late daytime tried their best to keep Dene out of the control room, where he was attempting to direct my every thought the first two weeks. He was so nervous because I wasn't a native New Yorker.

"And I found myself in that control room under a new name. I had gone by my real name, Sheila Mayhew, in Houston. But Dene thought people would misunderstand it as Sheila May, and he wanted to avoid anything that sounded too 'Southern country.' But what would my new name be? Dene and I hashed this out long distance, with me in Houston, one hand on the phone, the other in a suitcase. Dene was looking for something that said New York. He seriously considered Annie Knickerbocker (*Annie*, the musical, was very big back then). Fortunately, Dan Taylor intervened. I'm not sure why Dan thought of York. He probably just got tired of Dene and me going back and forth, each rejecting the other's suggestions. I can imagine him finally just throwing up his hands, 'Oh, for God's sake, just name her after the city!' And I have kept Sheila York as my professional name every since."

Lee Arnold hosted a 4th of July special for Mutual featuring Willie Nelson and Merle Haggard.

Ed Salamon

Mike Fitzgerald participated in an armadillo race at Rockaway Playland amusement park with WHN traffic reporter Judy Herron and others. He recalls that in order to get the armadillo to run, contestants had to blow air on the animal's butt through a straw.

In October, WHN announced that it was going to carry the Mets baseball games. WHN had broadcast the Mets games from 1972 through 1974, prior to the switch to country. Dene Hallam publicly expressed concern that listeners who tuned in to WHN for country music and heard baseball instead might listen to WKHK instead. However, he also conceded that Mets fans who listened to the games in the evenings might well keep WHN on their radios and listen in the mornings.

By this time, WHN was back to doing interviews with artists who appeared at the station, rather than guest deejay appearances. Sheila York recalls, "Even though I was rarely on during the daytime, I got to do interviews with quite a few visiting celebrities, including Willie Nelson, Glen Campbell, The Judds, George Strait, and Hank Williams, Jr. (who was brought in the back way—he was unpopular with some locals for derogatory things he'd said and sung about New York and the North). My favorite memory is Reba McEntire. I remember her as being the first interview I did. She was certainly among the first. I recall my sweaty hands and the trouble I had swallowing. I'd never done live interviews before. She'd only had a couple of hits back then, but I really admired her singing. I'd done my homework, asked Lee Arnold what he knew about her (he knew everything about everybody). So when she sat down, I could ask intelligent questions about *her*. And she ran with it. Within a couple of minutes, we were chatting like two high school girlfriends who hadn't seen each other in years."

CHAPTER ELEVEN
1983

"American Made" – Oak Ridge Boys (1983)

In February, Dene Hallam resigned as program director of WHN to program rival WKHK. Incredibly WHN, an AM music station, had survived direct format competition from an FM and was still beating WKHK after more than two years. Hallam would now use all the programming tricks that he had used successfully for WHN against his former station on an FM stereo frequency. "Sorry, Pal," as he would say. Music director Pam Green served as acting program director until Hallam's replacement was named.

In March, Joel Raab joined WHN as program director. Raab was a New Yorker who had begun in country radio as a part time air personality on WJJD in Chicago while attending Northwestern University. After graduation, he went to work at WEEP, Pittsburgh, when I was consulting the station. He succeeded Dene Hallam as program director there. Raab was therefore very familiar with the approach that Dene and I had taken with WHN. He then joined WHK, Cleveland, owned by Malrite, as program director. General manager Brian Moors said that I was the one who had introduced him to Raab, and noted that WABC had recently given up music for a talk format, leaving WHN one less competitor for music on the AM dial. WHN had therefore ultimately won the music battle over WABC, but by this time that contest was being fought on the FM dial. Hallam, Raab and I had all programmed WEEP in Pittsburgh (it was the first country station programmed by me and Raab, the second for Hallam).

That same month, Mutual ran an ad in the trades promoting Lee Arnold's new weekly network radio show *On A Country Road.*

WHN began to broadcast Mets baseball games. Most people in the industry at the time thought that country music and baseball worked well together. New York's earlier station, WJRZ, likewise had carried the Mets.

Mets baseball provided some of Shelia York's best memories of WHN: "I'm a baseball fan, and a National League fan. The Mets were just terrible when I came to New York. We used to joke that there was one good thing about a Mets game: you were only a half-inning away from Major League baseball. Then the Mets came to WHN and I got to ride with them all the way to the world championship. Baseball also affects my memories of WHN. For all the years the Mets were on WHN, I 'ran the board' for them at the station when they played during my shift, which was almost every weeknight and on Saturday afternoons. So a lot of my memories are tied to the Mets. General manager Rick Dames asked me to do 'features' for WHN's expanded pregame show during the playoffs and the World Series. I didn't have a producer, so I had to come up with the ideas, chase down the subject, get an interview, edit it. I'd never done that sort of thing before, and spent a lot of time being nauseous with nerves. But the show's hosts and staff were generous and helpful. And never let on that I was essentially out of my depth. I got my favorite Bob Costas story out of it. Bob was doing reporting for the pregame shows. About the same time, I got a call from a writer at NBC sports who was working on a new weekend sports show that was looking for female talent, and their latest interviewee hadn't known a thing about sports. You have to bear in mind that back then it was a lot harder to find women who knew sports and had on-camera skills. He'd heard something funny I'd said on the air that indicated I at least understood baseball. He wanted me to meet his boss and he set up an interview with the head of sports (who shall remain nameless). The writer ushered me into the meeting, and the head of sports could not have been ruder. I got maybe ten seconds, then he just walked out. The writer was mortified. I took it in stride, as I never really thought there was a chance, but shared the story with a few other people at WHN, including Bob. During a playoff game, I ran into Bob in the stands, sitting with the sports head. Bob stands up, waves me over, acts like I'm a longtime friend, and introduces me to the guy. 'Do you know Sheila?' It was the nicest thing a really famous person has ever done for me."

On April 18th, WHN celebrated its 10th anniversary in the country format with a gala at the New York State Theater in Lincoln Center. Pam Green recalls that Ronnie Milsap provided the entertainment in exchange for expenses only. "Milsap was a huge star then, so that was a coup." WHN staffers all received diamond pins from Tiffany in their famous blue boxes commemorating the event. Joel Raab, having just arrived from similarly named WHK, still is embarrassed that he naturally confused the call letters when he took the stage to talk about the station. Lee Arnold remembers that Alabama attended as guests and he introduced them to the attendees. RCA regional promotion executive Tim McFadden attended with his label's acts.

WHN producer Jim Nedelka recalls Willie Nelson celebrating his 50th birthday by appearing on Lee Arnold's show on April 30th. Arnold pointed out that it was appropriate since Willie Hugh Nelson's initials were WHN.

The air staff at this time consisted of Del De Montreux (mornings), Lee Arnold (middays), Mike Fitzgerald (early afternoons), Dan Taylor (afternoons), Shelia York (evenings) and Brian Kelly (overnights). Joel Raab would fill in on the air for vacations, illnesses and on an occasional Saturday morning, using his air name Jay Stevens. He remembers getting odd looks from staffers as they saw him in the studio through the big glass window that faces the hallway, since WHN management had seldom done air shifts. Later one of the salespersons who had not been in the station during Raab's shift asked him "who was that guy filling in for Lee Arnold today?" Raab asked, "What did you think of him?" The sales person responded "He's OK. He sounds like everybody else." Raab says he was relieved. One Saturday, he dedicated a song to a fictitious caller from a kosher deli. An astute listener called and said, "Shame on you; kosher delis aren't open on Saturdays." Raab is the son of a rabbi, so he really should have known better.

On July 2nd, Willie Nelson held his annual Willie Nelson 4th of July Picnic concert at Giants Stadium in Rutherford, New Jersey. Previously held in Texas and Oklahoma, at this point New York was enough of a country music market to be the location for this event. The ten hour concert also included outlaws Merle Haggard, Waylon Jennings and Mr. Jennings's wife, Jessi Colter.

CHAPTER TWELVE
1984

"Thank God For The Radio" – The Kendalls (1984)

When the ratings came out in January, WHN had been beaten by WKHK. They almost equally split the 4% share of audience that WHN once had, with WKHK winning only by a hair. It had taken WKHK three years in the country format to beat WHN, a feat that was usually immediate in direct format competition between FM and AM stations. However, as soon as the ratings were announced, WKHK dropped the country format to become "Lite FM 106.7 WLTW," a soft adult contemporary station. WLTW featured artists like Barbra Streisand, Frank Sinatra and the Carpenters. The station also played softer songs from such artists as Elton John, Elvis Presley and the Beatles. Viacom national program director Bill Figenshu was quoted as saying that WKHK "tanked badly," and attributed it to the fact that "country is not in New Yorkers' DNA." Of course that doesn't consider the success that WHN had. WHN again had the country format all to itself in New York.

Pam Green recalls the Judds first visit to WHN: " I remember when the Judds made their first appearance at WHN. They were guest deejays. They told me that they didn't like New York City. It was probably their first trip here. They were promoting their first single 'I Had A Dream.' I think they probably ended up liking New York City, as they made many more trips over the years. Naomi and Wynonna are good friends of mine today."

Ellen Zucker began working at WHN that year as the front desk receptionist. She recalls how business people who worked in the building on Park Avenue in midtown Manhattan would stare at the country music artists who came to visit WHN dressed in cowboy boots and hats.

Lee Arnold won the Academy of Country Music's award as 1983 Country Deejay of the Year.

In October, Mutual sold WHN to Doubleday Broadcasting for $13 million, three million dollars less than their 1980 purchase price. Doubleday was also the owner of the New York Mets baseball team and Mets games were carried on WHN. Doubleday's president was Gary Stevens.

After the sale, Lee Arnold continued doing his weekly show *Lee Arnold On A Country Road* as well as specials for Mutual Broadcasting.

Mike Fitzgerald began hosting *Solid Gold Country* for the United Stations radio network.

Ronnie Milsap receives his diamond "10" pin at the April 18, 1983 party at the New York State Theater in Lincoln Center celebrating WHN's decade as a country radio station. Shown are Pam Green, program director Joel Raab, general manager Brian Moors, Milsap, Mutual Broadcasting president/CEO Marty Rubenstein and sales manager Mike Valentino. (Courtesy Joel Raab)

A WHN began carrying Mets baseball games in 1983 and would broadcast the team's games for the remainder the station's existence. It produced bumper stickers which promoted both the Mets and WHN's country format.

John Denver, whose music was played on WHN earlier and more frequently than on other country stations, visits with Pam Green, Joel Raab, Dan Taylor and Lee Arnold at the Park Avenue studios in April 1984. (Courtesy Pam Green)

Willie Nelson is welcomed to the opening night of a five day stand at Radio City Music Hall in October 1984 by WAPP/WHN vice president general manager Pat McNally, Joel Raab and director of creative services for WAPP/WHN, Susan Storms.

Doubleday Broadcasting acquired WHN in October 1984. Although WHN no longer held a No. 2 position in the New York market, it was still "the most listened to country music station in the nation" according to this trade ad. (Courtesy Peter Kanze)

Glen Campbell holds Pam Green and Sheila York on his lap during a December 1984 visit to WHN promoting his new single "A Lady Like You". (Courtesy Pam Green)

Tom Wopat, who played Luke Duke on *The Dukes of Hazzard* television show visits with Del De Montreux and Pam Green at WHN in the Kaufman Astoria Studios in January 1987. Wopat had begun recording the previous year and "The Rock And Roll Of Love", which was to become his biggest hit, was then climbing the country charts. (Courtesy Pam Green)

CHAPTER THIRTEEN
1985

"Who's Gonna Fill Their Shoes" – George Jones (1985)

General manager Brian Moors left WHN. Pat McNally, WAPP's vice president and general manager now served in that capacity for both stations.

On April 24th, McNally, Joel Raab and director of creative services for WAPP/WHN, Susan Storms, welcomed Willie Nelson to the opening night of a five day stand at Radio City Music Hall.

In May, Ruth Meyer re-joined WHN, this time in the newly created position of station manager. Meyer had been named program director of WHN shortly after its switch to country. Before that, Meyer had been program director of Top 40 WMCA. Gary Stevens, now president of Doubleday, WHN's owner, had been one of her WMCA deejays.

Over the years, many people have told me that Meyer got frustrated whenever she asked why things were done a certain way and received the response "that's the way Ed Salamon taught us to do it." One day she put a piece of paper with my name on a vacant office door, telling the staff "if Ed Salamon is still so involved with the station, he should have an office here."

Joel Raab left WHN and formed a consultancy, Joel Raab Associates, but recalls that his final rating book with the station was the last time that WHN would have a three share with 12+ listeners and ranked eighth among adults 24-54. Raab was quoted saying he was gratified that he was able to make baseball work with country music.

Mike Fitzgerald left the station and was not immediately replaced.

In August, Ruth Meyer hired Neal "Moon" Mullins from WDAF, Kansas City, as program director. Mullins said that he planned to include more oldies as well as more songs in general in an effort aimed at expanding the station's audience base.

The WHN air staff, when Mullins joined, was Del De Montreux (mornings), Lee Arnold (middays), Dan Taylor (afternoons), Sheila York (nights) and Stan Martin (overnights). Carol Mason and Ian Carr did weekends and fill-in.

Mullin's office was a large suite with a window facing Park Avenue, which was formerly the general manager's office. By then, the sales offices had moved to the Met Life Building (formerly known as the Pan Am Building) at 200 Park Avenue.

Mullins recalls that Meyer tried, but could not get the budget to recreate the WHN family picnic which was held the year the station adopted the country format.

In September, WHN won *Billboard*'s award as Country Station of the Year.

The Highwaymen were a country super group consisting of Johnny Cash, Willie Nelson, Kris Kristofferson and Waylon Jennings. The group's name was taken from the title track of their first album, which became a No. 1 country single in 1985. Dan Taylor remembers emceeing their show at Radio City Music Hall: "When I came off stage, they were all in the wings. The normally quiet Johnny Cash said 'Alright! That's the way to do it, son. That's getting them goin',' at the top of his voice. It scared the hell out of me, since I've never seen him so animated."

Big River with words and music by country artist Roger Miller opened on Broadway. It was based on Mark Twain's *The*

Adventures of Huckleberry Finn. It would receive seven Tony awards.

In December, former WMCA "Good Guy" Dan Daniel returned to WHN, taking Mike Fitzgerald's slot.

Ian Carr, who had worked at WNOE in New Orleans, was surprised at the latitude WHN personalities had in their presentations. Carr recalls, "New Orleans was the 33rd market at the time and WNOE was about as tightly formatted as a station could be. In fact, their slogan was 'More Country / Less Bull.' I was expecting WHN to be even tougher. When I asked Neal how I should run the show, he said 'well . . . it's pretty simple. Talk between every other song (at least) . . . and make sure you have something interesting to say. That's it.'"

CHAPTER FOURTEEN
1986

"Will The Wolf Survive" – Waylon Jennings (1986)

Rick Nelson died in a plane crash on New Year's Eve. Pam Green and Dan Taylor came in to the station on that holiday to produce a memorial special that ran on New Year's Day. Nelson had been a guest deejay for the first time on WHN and the station had played many of his 50s and 60s hits, as well as his New York inspired "Garden Party."

Newcomer Ian Carr was allowed to change the format of his show. Carr recalls, "After a few weeks of doing Sunday night shows, I approached Neal about doing something different with the time slot. I think my pitch was 'Sunday night is kind of a lost shift. I think I can do something interesting with it.' Hey . . . youth makes you bold. Anyway, I suggested that we do a call-in joke show and Neal gave me the green light to try it. Imagine that? A twenty-two year old kid with two weeks in the big city under his belt and the PD is letting me do my thing! Neal was cool. We called it 'Sunday Funnies.' The show was a hit, doubling the ratings for that daypart. It was also extremely difficult to produce. In between playing music I would take calls, record them to tape, edit them as necessary, and cue them up for playback. I had an intern, Joan Chin, who helped with the show. In one of those strange ways that life runs in circles, twenty years later I found myself on Sirius Satellite Radio co-hosting essentially the same show with Jackie Martling. Even some of the jokes are the same. The weirdest part of the story was that, on my first day, I ran into Joan Chin, who's now producing for Sirius."

In March, trade publications broke the news that Indianapolis based Emmis Broadcasting had agreed to purchase WHN, along with WAPP and WAVA-FM, in the Washington, D.C. market, for $53 million. The sale was handled by former Doubleday president Gary Stevens, now a first president at Wertheim and Company, a media broker. As part of the deal, it was reported that WHN had agreed to continue to carry the Mets. Emmis president, Jeff Smulyan, was quoted as saying they would be doing market research to determine where they would take their new outlets, and that the company would strive to keep current management intact. The future of country radio in New York was again in question.

In April, Gary Havens, a consultant and programmer best known as program director of WIRE in Indianapolis, was hired by Emmis head of programming, Rick Cummings, to evaluate an idea Smulyan had to make WHN an all-sports station. Havens says that Rick was a college friend at Butler University and they had both served as ushers in each other's weddings. Havens had previously worked with Cummings on some consulting jobs for WENS-FM, Indianapolis, and other projects. After three or four days listening to the market, he reported that all-sports would be a huge risk. There had never been an all-sports radio station. However, he felt that WHN, as New York's only country station, still had potential with some tweaking. Havens met with Smulyan, Cummings and Rick Dames, who was to be the station's new general manager, and they discussed the possibility of him joining the station as program director.

Pam Green remembers that Willie Nelson helped her celebrate her birthday on July 8th: "He was a guest deejay that day.

The staff gave me a cake and he presented it to me. He also signed my birthday card. It was a pretty special day for me. Willie was one of the artists that always came in the 54th Street entrance to 400 Park Avenue. That entrance was usually locked. I would go down to meet him and bring him and his team up. I arranged with the building manager. Because we heavily promoted an appearance by a guest deejay fans would be waiting outside the building for them."

In July 1986, Doubleday moved WHN's facilities out of Manhattan to Kaufman Astoria Studios, 34-12 36th Street, in Astoria, Queens along with WQHT (formerly WAPP). WHN maintained a sales office in Manhattan.

Kaufman Astoria Studios were built in 1920. The first two Marx Brothers films *The Cocoanuts* (1929) and *Animal Crackers* (1930) were shot there. The building had also been known as Astoria Studio and Paramount Studio. Other motion pictures filmed there include the musicals *Hair* and *The Wiz*, *Goodfellas* and *Carlito's Way*. Many television shows, including *Sesame Street* originated at Kaufman Astoria. In 1984, The Jacksons' music video "Torture" was filmed there.

Pam Green remembers, "I had a big office because I was in the music library. But we didn't have any windows. 400 Park Avenue was our long time address. Literally, you had any food you wanted within walking distance and some of the best restaurants around. When we moved to Astoria, there wasn't much. We normally ordered food from the cafeteria. The menu rarely changed and the food was not good. Getting to Astoria was not much fun. Since I lived on the Upper East Side, getting to 400 Park Avenue was easy, but when we moved, getting to work became problematic. There was a jitney that ran between 53rd and Third Avenue to Astoria round trip. I remember the driver was a nice man by the name of Ralph. He took good care of us, but if we weren't on time the jitney would leave without us. A few times I would call the front desk at Astoria Studios and asked them to tell the driver to please hold it for me—I was on my way and they usually did. But one night, I guess I was too late. I had to take the subway around 6:30 or 7:00 pm. I may have taken the subway once or twice but that was it. I had to ask directions to the subway and did find it. I was by myself and it was the most nerve-wracking night of my life. I was on the upper subway platform by myself. I had to pass a bunch of guys who were hanging out and didn't look like they were getting on a train. I thought for sure something would happen like they would mug me. Luckily, nothing happened."

"Many mornings when the jitney arrived at the Astoria Studios, we would pull up behind a station wagon with a bunch of kids in there. It was Woody Allen, Mia Farrow and their kids. Woody would be there to film. Other than that, we rarely saw any celebrities besides the country artists that would come out to Astoria to be guest deejays. We were spoiled by Park Avenue. Astoria was no Park Avenue. On Park Avenue, I could easily run over to Bloomingdale's or Saks Fifth Avenue to do a little shopping. There was no shopping in Astoria. I rarely got out of my office to go outside."

Sheila York recalls, "This is when I knew WHN would not last long. When the owners send you to hunker down in a cramped, damp, plastic-and-prefab space at the end of an echoing basement labyrinth in the Queens of the mid-1980s, you know their priorities have changed. It was obvious their energies were concentrated on the FM side and we were being propped up till they could decide what else to do with the station. Rumors were fresh every day. I thought the staff behaved with remarkable character under the circumstances."

The August 23rd issue of *Billboard* announced the Emmis Broadcasting Corporation was in the process of finalizing a $53 million purchase which included WAPP-FM, New York, WAVA-FM, Washington D.C. and WHN. The same article noted that WHN program director Neal "Moon" Mullins had resigned to start his own consultancy, with WHN as the first client. The new program director of WHN was Gary Havens, who had visited WHN in 1978, and emulated the programming and research strategies he saw at the station at WIRE, Indianapolis, where he was program director. Where Moon Mullins had expanded the playlist, Havens recalls his aim was "to play more hits and songs by well known country artists, while editing the fantastic air staff down to fewer and better live bits filled with real entertainment value." The air staff still consisted of Del De Montreux, Lee Arnold, Dan Daniel, Dan Taylor, Shelia York and Stan Martin. Mullins stayed through the end of the month to help with the transition.

When Emmis took over, Pat McNally left and was replaced by Rick Dames. McNally became general manager at KFRC, San Francisco.

The WHN offices were in the sub-basement of the Kaufman Astoria Studios. Reputedly, the basement corner was the former site of a giant swimming pool that was used in the 1940s Esther Williams movies. Havens describes the offices as, "kind of a rabbit warren of cubbyholes with studios made in a pre-fabricated dropped in fashion." It was an adjustment for the staff to work 40 feet below ground, and Havens had a camera put in so that the air staff could observe the weather at street level from the studio.

Unlike the mid 70s when WHN employed request line operators to field listener calls, at this point the deejays themselves were answering the request lines. Ian Carr recalls, "There were some memorable regular callers. My favorite was Myrtle. Myrtle had a distinctive, screechy voice. When she'd call I'd say 'Hi, Myrtle' and she'd reply 'How'd you know it was me?' Myrtle was always promising to send me a picture and one day she did. The photo was of a good looking African American woman standing on a sidewalk holding a baby. It looked like it was taken in the 50s. All the parked cars were of that era and the photo was black and white. When Myrtle called, she asked me if I got the picture. I said 'Yes, but I think it's kinda old.' 'No it isn't,' she replied. 'Myrtle, you're holding a baby in the photo.' 'Yes, yes I am.' 'How old is that baby now?' Then, in her screechy voice she nonchalantly said 'Well, he must be thirty-five or forty years old.' Gotta love Myrtle."WHN participated in the Marlboro Country Music Talent Roundup. Participants were invited to submit tapes and WHN received thousands of entries which were screened by Havens, Pam Green, creative services director Susan Storms and programming staffer Maggie Day. Finalists performed for judges at the Bottom Line. On November 8th the winners, the Surreal McCoys, performed with Alabama, Merle Haggard and Ricky Skaggs at the Meadowlands. Their usual venue was Joe's Bar on 6th Street in Manhattan. Joe's had no cover charge, served two dollar beers, had Christmas lights strung on the ceiling all year long and mounted deer heads on the wall.

Havens recalls the fall ratings as being in the low two shares, but because the New York market had such a large population, the cume listening still placed the station among country stations with the most listeners.

CHAPTER FIFTEEN
1987

"Forever And Ever Amen" – Randy Travis (1987)

WHN conducted a major contest targeted to listeners in the outer boroughs, Long Island and New Jersey. More than a million direct mail pieces were sent to homes in targeted zip codes. If listeners heard their names called on the air, they could win $100, $1000 or $100,000. The contest was syndicated by Jack McCoy, best known for his "The Last Contest" promotion. Jack recorded the contest promos at WHN in his distinctive, dramatic style. Havens says that, "although a lot of money was spent and the results were good, they were not good enough."

Del De Montreux did a live broadcast of the morning show from Giants Stadium in Rutherford, New Jersey when the Giants returned home as Super Bowl XXI winners after defeating Denver. De Montreux also originated his morning show from St. Petersburg, Florida, during the Mets spring training. The station hosted several sales junkets to the training center for advertisers in March.

In April, on the opening day of the Mets season, Gary Havens left WHN. Havens, who, with partners, owned two radio stations in West Virginia, had the opportunity to buy a full power station in Indianapolis. He had disclosed this to Emmis, who asked him to remain at WIIN through the winter ratings period.

Pam Green again acted as program director. Without Haven's advocacy for country, the decision was made to switch the station to all sports.

Pam Green recalls the day Emmis announced that it was changing WHN's format. "We were all gathered in a room at the Astoria Film studios where WHN had moved to. Jeff Smulyan, Rick Dames and Doyle Rose came to deliver the big announcement that WHN was going all sports."

Sheila York remembers "One evening, after the announcement had been made that WHN would soon be history, I was running a baseball game and had some free time during a long inning to stretch my legs. On a desk in the common area outside an executive office, right there in an in-box, was a stack of WFAN contracts. What the heck, I riffled them. I couldn't believe what I was seeing. The salaries were enormous by WHN standards. I thought, how are they going to pay for this? As it turned out, they had a lot of trouble that first year or so, till they found the right man for the contract: Don Imus. I confess I called a buddy who was signing on to do a weekend sports commentary show to tell him what those other people were making, just in case he hadn't signed his own contract yet.

"I spent a lot of time thinking about what would come after the end of WHN. I was given a courtesy interview by John Chanin, the new WFAN program director, but I didn't have the depth of sports knowledge that would be required. I started to think about whether I wanted to stay in radio . . . and whether it would be possible. Not many people give up their New York City radio jobs willingly, and New York didn't have much turnover on the stations whose music I could deejay. Club music was big, but I knew I'd never be able to convince any program director I was fond of clubs."

Duane Allen of the Oak Ridge Boys recalls that the station was still strong enough to mobilize New York's country fans: "One of the most important events in our career came in 1987.

WHN: WHEN NEW YORK CITY WENT COUNTRY

The Oak Ridge Boys headlined Radio City Music Hall for five sold-out shows. Our supporting act was the Judds, who were just breaking. WHN was the major media sponsor of our show and every show was an event. The city was buzzing with press interviews, TV and radio interviews and all kinds of after show parties. We still mark that as one of our more successful run of dates in New York City. WHN got the word out for us and together we rocked the Big Apple."

On July 1st, 1987, Dan Taylor played Ray Price's country/pop crossover hit from 1970, "For The Good Times" and for the last time said, "this is WHN, New York." The station then became Sports Radio, WFAN.

Sheila York was there. "I have a few very clear memories of that last day, July 1st, which was (and is) my birthday. I returned to the station to be there at 3pm for the switch from WHN to WFAN. I can recall standing on the other side of the studio window, watching Dan Taylor signing off like a champ, and then hearing Suzyn Waldman over the speaker uttering the first live words on 'The Fan' from another studio.

"I know Suzie has said publicly since that she looked out the window of the news studio where she was and people were holding hands and crying. I don't recall that at all. There might have been some misty eyes. And maybe one or two shed a tear. After all, it was the end. But we'd had plenty of time to prepare for it, and I don't recall any mass weeping or widespread display of emotion. I'm pretty sure most of us felt strongly we weren't going to go all mushy in front of those WFAN guys.

"I recall chatting with Howie Rose afterward, about what he'd be doing for WFAN, but mostly about his personal life—he was getting married to Barbara. I'm so glad to see how Howie's career has flourished. He's one of the aces in the business.

"I also recall the awkwardness with other members of the new team, even though we all tried to act normal, be gracious. I think they felt more awkward than we did. They wanted to

Ed Salamon

cheer, but could hardly, in front of us. But ultimately, the room was full of strangers.

"I recall after maybe ten minutes of chatting, a hug here and there, and the promise most of us knew we'd never keep to 'stay in touch,' walking alone down that empty, cavernous corridor to the elevator, and out of the basement into a bright July afternoon. I was going to continue to do commercials, see if there was any chance of starting an acting career at age 37 (there wasn't) and see if I could write the book I'd been thinking about (I eventually did)."

York then spent a few years doing commercials both on and off camera (and one brief stint as a part-timer at WNSR) before taking a sharp career turn and joining a financial firm in the mid-1990s, where she still works, as a supervisory analyst (she notes that she had nothing to do with the mortgage crisis). She is also a successful author of fiction.

Dan Taylor remembers "The last day was a sad one. I couldn't believe I was bestowed the responsibility of saying goodbye to historic call letters that were sixty years old. I was starting another job a couple days later across the street at 66 WNBC so I tried to mentally treat it as just another day, but it wasn't. It was a most emotional event. As Larry Gatlin's song 'I've Done Enough Dyin' Today' ended, I made a signoff speech with everyone gathered in the studio, before playing the Ray Price song ('For the Good Times'). I chose that as the final song because when you listen to the lyrics, it seems the most appropriate. Then I punched the button to fire off the last tape cartridge of a WHN ID jingle, which I gave to my good friend who produced it—Jon Wolfert at JAM. A nervous 'board op' said 'Do you wanna hit the first thing for WFAN?' I politely said 'No thanks, it's all yours' and left for a big party at my dear friend Lee Arnold's home. It was weird driving there knowing I'd never say those great call letters again. A lot of great memories and I was only twenty-eight years old. And yes, I still have the tape cartridge of that last song I played by Ray Price sitting in my home studio."

Music director Pam Green and air personality Del De Montreux were constants during WHN's country years. Lee Arnold was there at the beginning and end, and was there most of the time in between.

All of us who were program directors benefitted from their knowledge, hard work and dedication. The only other constants during WHN's country years that I recall were engineers Joe Ellis, Larry Finkle, Tommy Franken, Julius McEachern and Dick James. Others staffers came and went, but they were there for the duration.

Fifteen hours before WHN changed to all-sports, adult contemporary station WYNY at 97.1 dropped its format after about ten years and switched to country music. This gave New York an FM county station for the first time since WKHK. WYNY kicked off the format with Dolly Parton's "Think About Love," a 1986 No. 1 country hit.

Ironically, Howie Rose, whom I had hired in 1977 to replace Bill Mazur as WHN's sports director, became one of the station's first talk show hosts on WFAN, continuing some of the WHN tradition.

During its fifteen years in the country music format, WHN amassed an incredible library of country records. During the six years that I was there, music was played from taped carts that looked a lot like eight track tapes. The records would be recorded on the carts and, as the carts wore out or broke, would need to be recorded again. Pam Green usually was able to obtain multiple copies of each sigle and album for the library. Many people wondered what happened to them. Moon Mullins recalls that Iuka, Mississippi based country consultant Rusty Walker was working with WHN at this time and bought the library. "It cost him $8,000 to ship it to Mississippi!," says Moon, who notes that Walker would later be hired to consult WYNY.

Ed Salamon

On September 22, 1985, WYNY switched frequency with sister station WQHT, moving to 103.5. The station remained country until February 4, 1996. A few days later, it became WKTU, a dance oriented contemporary hit music station.

On December 7, 1996, Big City Radio began a country simulcast on WGRX, Briarcliff, New York, WWHB, Hampton Bays, New York and WZVU, Long Branch, New Jersey. The three stations, known as Y-107, were all at 107.1 and attempted to cover most of the New York market. Two years later, WRNJ, Belvidere, New Jersey was added to the simulcast. On May 7, 2002, the stations changed to a Spanish language format.

On January 21, 2013, country radio returned to the New York City market on a facility recently acquired by Cumulus Media. The station was formerly Christian formatted WFME, owned by Family Radio and licensed to Newark, New Jersey. After temporarily using the call letters WRXP, the call letters were changed to WNSH and the station identified as Nash FM 94.7.

ABOUT THE AUTHOR

My interest in radio and music began in my pre-school days with the RCA combination radio and phonograph that was the source of entertainment in our home on Nixon Street in Pittsburgh's Manchester neighborhood. My parents allowed me to play their 78 rpm records and bought me a few "kiddie records" of my own, but I gravitated to the music I heard on the radio.

My parents would have to tune in specific programs like *The Lone Ranger* for me. When I was on my own with the dial, I usually wound up listening to the first station on the dial that came in clearly, 860 WHOD, because it was the easiest to find. That station carried a variety of programming, but the most memorable music was played in the late afternoon by deejay Porky Chedwick. Soon I was begging my parents to buy me records he played like "Maybelline" by Chuck Berry.

When we got a television, I was introduced to country music via local acts, including Slim Bryant and the Wild Cats and Abbie Neal and Her Ranch Girls, who appeared on many of the local shows.

By the time I was in high school, I was deejaying record hops. At that time, most high schools and youth groups held dances. In Pittsburgh, kids favored songs that were good to dance to, whether or not they were hit records. Deejays including Chedwick, Bob Mack, Mad Mike Metrovich, Terry

201

Ed Salamon

Lee, Charlie Apple and Zeke Jackson played obscure records that were popular at dances on smaller AM stations surrounding Pittsburgh. This music became known as "Pittsburgh oldies." I learned that the best records were not necessarily the ones that became hits. Pittsburgh's leading Top 40 station, KQV, was being steered by legendary programmer John Rook. I absorbed the nuances of the Top 40 format by listening to that station.

At the same time I was playing in a garage band. My group, the Headliners, were used by radio deejays for a live music segment at their record hops. We worked for KQV deejays Chuck Brinkman and Dex Allen, WZUM's Johnny Walker and Al Gee and WAMO's Porky Chedwick. By the time I realized that a music career was not my future, I had made a number of contacts in radio.

KDKA hired me as assistant promotion director and marketing research director when I graduated from college on the strength of my public relations skills learned working for a Congressman, for whom I wrote press releases and letters. When the station's music director left, I offered to do that job in addition for free. It was a time when those in radio got their greatest satisfaction from sharing music that they were passionate about with their listeners. When KDKA's audience got larger and younger (adult contemporary formatted KDKA, perennially No. 1 in total audience, was even the No. 2 teen station while I was music director), I was hired as program director by country formatted WEEP, also in Pittsburgh, which was seeking a younger audience. I saw a greater opportunity there and that station's success led to me being hired to program WHN.

After WHN, I began a twenty year run as head of programming for a succession of radio networks. The United Stations, a partnership with Dick Clark, two other Mutual Broadcast System employees and me, acquired the RKO Radio Network, merged with the Transtar Radio Network to form Unistar. Viacom, which owned CBS, bought Unistar and competitor Westwood One and merged them and the non-news operations of CBS radio into Westwood One, and I became president/programming of Westwood One, which was the largest radio network at the time.

When my contract expired in 2002, I moved to Nashville to serve as Executive Director of the Country Radio Broadcasters, the non-profit organization that presents the radio and music industry convention, the Country Radio Seminar. After seven years there, I briefly ran a record label and music publishing company. I have taught at Belmont University and Middle Tennessee State University and authored *Pittsburgh's Golden Age of Radio* (Arcadia Publishing).

About the Type

This book was set in Times. The Times font was drawn by Victor Lardent, an advertising artist for the *Times of London*, under the supervision of typographer Stanley Morison of Monotype, a British font foundry. The font was initially released in 1932.

Designed by John Taylor-Convery
Composed at JTC Imagineering, Santa Maria, CA